CHAOTIC
HAPPINESS

The Psychology of Finding Yourself
in a World That's Lost

CHAOTIC
HAPPINESS

The Psychology of Finding Yourself in a World That's Lost

TJ HOEGH, MS, NCC, LPC

Publisher Mike Sanders
Senior Editor Alexandra Andrzejewski
Art Director William Thomas
Senior Designer Jessica Lee
Development Editor Augustin Kendall
Illustrator Yiffy Gu
Proofreaders Georgette Beatty, Lorraine Martindale
Indexer Beverlee Day

First American Edition, 2022
Published in the United States by DK Publishing
6081 E. 82nd Street, Indianapolis, IN 46250

22 23 24 25 26 10 9 8 7 6 5 4 3 2
001-326908-APR2022

Therapy examples shared throughout the book represent a culmination
of anonymous case studies and do not reflect the story of any individual clients
or their families.

Published in the United States by Dorling Kindersley Limited.

Library of Congress Catalog Number: 2021944247
ISBN: 978-0-7440-5127-8

DK books are available at special discounts when purchased in bulk for sales
promotions, premiums, fund-raising, or educational use. For details, contact:
SpecialSales@dk.com

Printed and bound in Canada

For the curious
www.dk.com

CONTENTS

AUTHOR LETTER

Life is chaotic, and far too often the hardships of the world outweigh the things that bring us joy. The ability to make our way through the chaos and find happiness is essential for our well-being, but so few of us do it well. I'd like to help you with this, if you'll let me. As a therapist, helping people beat the odds and overcome the chaos is what I'm best at.

Our challenges are never the same, but they share a common theme. The difficulties we encounter come from living in a directionless, unpredictable, and uncertain world. It's this reality that we sometimes run from, largely because we can't change it. Accidents will continue to happen, people will get sick, and so on. In some shape or form, there will always be tragedy that exists in the world, but when we can rise above the chaos, we can reclaim our happiness.

As we move forward, I'd like to help you identify some of the unique challenges in your world and give you a guide that might help you face them. These are things I talk about with my clients, and they're things that I personally live by, too.

The following pages outline the collective chaos we all face and some rules to live by as you continue the fight in finding your own happiness. And make no mistake . . . you will have to fight for it. The fight for happiness is one that too many of us have failed to win, but what I've seen and what I've experienced shows me that it's possible if we keep fighting the battle. That's exactly what I'm asking you to do with me.

TJ Hoegh
@tik_tok_counseling

HAPPINESS IN A CHAOTIC WORLD

The world is a chaotic place—there's no way of getting around that. As much as we try to create order in our lives, the reality is that most of our existence is dependent upon the disorder of a world indifferent to our efforts. This is just the inevitable truth of being alive. When you're interviewing for a new job, you could do everything you can to plan out your talking points but fail to notice a mustard stain on your shirt that ultimately leaves the lasting impression. When you're starting a new relationship, you might find that you remind the other person of someone they used to know, someone maybe they didn't like. These are just a couple of examples of the disorder we can't avoid or prevent.

If there's so much that can't be controlled, what are we supposed to do? Float through this existence defeated and distraught? Obviously, the answer is no. Even if we don't always know how to deal with the chaos in the world, we have to find a way to move through it. Charles Bukowski once said, "What matters most is how well you walk through the fire." How well do you walk through the fire? Typically, as we get older and wiser, we all inevitably learn how to survive the fires of life. But sometimes surviving the fire takes all the energy we have; sometimes surviving isn't enough.

"Just surviving" doesn't bring happiness, and often "just surviving" seems like the only option for many people. This is clearly demonstrated in the way we talk to each other on a daily basis. When we say "I'm not too bad" or "I'm hanging in there," it's pretty obvious that avoiding disaster is our only expectation sometimes. And it's true that surviving is something we need to aim for, and just getting through the day is an accomplishment. But what if we could find our happiness inside of the chaos? If we could learn how to do this, we'd use these challenges we're facing as opportunities for finding deeper levels of happiness.

The more profound the challenges we face, the more profound it is when we find a way to rise above them. It's a special kind of happiness when you achieve so much in this world that gives you so little. These victories taste a little bit sweeter because you get to look yourself in the mirror and say, "I did this. It was the strength in me that got me past what I was facing." I like to call this experience "chaotic happiness" because it's born in the fire of the persistent fight we're constantly waging against a world where the odds of finding joy are not always stacked in our favor.

You might be thinking, "This is all just talk" and wonder how can you actually seize this chaotic happiness for yourself. This is where the three rules of chaotic happiness come into play. I developed these rules after working with clients who were also trying to find it for themselves. As a psychotherapist, I've spent the majority of my time doing crisis intervention in prisons, in psychiatric hospitals, and in communities with people in extreme circumstances. I've found that helping people find happiness in the chaos of life is the thing in this world I'm best at, and these rules I've created will guide you in your own journey as you fight the fires of life by finding the fire within.

I believe in the process I've created because I've seen it work in my clients' lives. Life is so unfair to all of us in so many ways, without exception. I've never met a person who hasn't been deeply hurt by the world's insufferable ability to stare us down and break us badly. I used to think that being crushed was the only outcome that could come from the world. After all, if these challenges are unchangeable, the results of them must be, too. But I've learned that it's the best in ourselves—compassion, understanding, and strength—that can arise from within us in the toughest of times. We can't change the challenges that come from the chaos, but we can change ourselves.

EXISTENTIAL ANXIETY

I love a good underdog story, don't you? And make no mistake, we are the underdogs here. I believe it's you and me and everyone else against the chaos, and happiness is a hard-won prize. The path to realizing chaotic happiness is a treacherous one . . . one that you're never really done with. So, if you're going to come along with me, be prepared for some stumbling and strife. But I promise you this: If you commit to learning these rules with me, you'll find things in yourself that will help you for the rest of your life. As the old saying goes, "Give someone a fish, you'll feed them for a day. Teach them how to fish, you'll feed them for life." I want to teach you to fish, not give you one-size-fits-all answers that will leave you hungry later. I want to help you find a new way of being for yourself that will help protect your happiness no matter what the world throws at you.

However, before we outline how to tackle the challenges that come from the chaos, let's take a deeper look at what's creating all this chaos in the first place: the uncharted, unpredictable, and uncertain world we live in. Once we better understand these challenging aspects, we'll be better prepared to combat them with each of the three rules of chaotic happiness.

In psychology, it's these three aspects of the world that cause what we refer to as "existential anxiety," or our fear that our lives are inherently pointless. Existential anxiety is found at

the root of all the challenges we face on a daily basis through, well, existing. Imagine what life would be like if the world was charted, predictable, and certain—a world where you always knew what to do and could anticipate every single thing that would happen. Everything you wanted was guaranteed. If the world was like this, there wouldn't be problems. Life would be simple, and being happy would be easy.

Sadly, we know the world is not this way. In order to find happiness, we all need to learn how to confront the anxiety that comes from existing in the uncharted, unpredictable, and uncertain universe. By addressing our existential anxiety, we're fortifying the foundation from which all of life's challenges stem. By addressing our existential anxiety, we set ourselves up for profound, lasting happiness.

UNCHARTED

In the chaotic universe, no path is laid out for us. We have complete freedom to choose what we do. Life doesn't come with an instruction book, and this is a daunting reality. How do we know what we're supposed to do? What if a choice leads to something terrible? Much of our anxiety comes from having a directionless existence.

Have you ever had to make a difficult decision, such as choosing a side in an argument or selecting an academic path or career that had life-altering consequences? Then you have experienced the existential anxiety that comes from living in the uncharted. Unlimited freedom in making choices and a lack of direction cause a ton of stress.

When you made those difficult choices, did you worry about whether you made the right one, or maybe even whether there was a "right" choice to begin with? We do this because we want the security of knowing we've done the best possible thing that will have the best possible outcome. The dilemma here is that we'll never have such verification. There will always be what-ifs, and we need to learn to deal with this.

The key to dealing with this uncharted territory is finding yourself and determining your own direction. The first rule of chaotic happiness accomplishes this. When you know who you are and where you want to go, suddenly it matters less that the world is inherently without direction. Having a secure sense of self and knowing what direction you want to take plays a major role in happiness. Without it, you're at risk of wandering about aimless and unsatisfied. I'll walk you through the first rule later in this chapter.

UNPREDICTABLE

No matter what we do, something unforeseen might throw us off our chosen path. The chaotic world is unpredictable. Not only are there no clear directions for life, but there are also no clear ways of knowing what will happen. It's this not knowing what might happen that becomes a huge barrier for a lot of people. This is largely because when we can't see the future, by default we imagine the worst. "What if I fail?" "What if the pain of not succeeding breaks me?" "What if what's on the other side of this decision is something unexpectedly awful?" These questions and the existential anxiety they bring are a significant part of what makes our external and internal world chaotic.

Our inability to know what might happen affects our peace of mind on a daily basis, and there's nothing we can do to be ready for the unpredictable things the world might throw at us. What we can do, though, is find people to surround us who can help us when life does bring unexpected challenges. The best way to combat the unpredictable is to create an environment with as much stability as possible, and the best place to start in creating this space is fostering healthy relationships that create a supportive environment.

To find happiness in our unpredictable world, you'll need to find the right people and develop strong relationships. It's these relationships that will be your constant when nothing else is. On your most difficult days, so much of your heartache

comes from challenges you never even imagined; you'll need good people there for you to help get through the tough times. This is what the second rule of chaotic happiness helps you with, and we'll talk more in depth about it later. However, for now, let's address the last aspect of the world that makes it a chaotic, challenging place to exist.

UNCERTAIN

Not only is the world uncharted and unpredictable, but it's also a place where there's nothing you can be totally sure of. When you've decided who you want to be and where you'd like to go, there's no guarantee you'll get there. This is so troublesome because people like to have reassurance. We all want to have the energy and effort we put into things rewarded, or at the very least not punished. The world has other plans, though, and when you are uncertain about whether the things you are doing are truly consequential, it's easy to get stuck in one place or resigned to "not trying very hard" for fear that it will all be for nothing.

The biggest problem with uncertainty is its tendency to immobilize your decisions. The solution to this problem is finding your purpose. By deciding what gives your life meaning, you free yourself from the external constraints of needing validation because you're getting your validation from within. When you decide with certainty what success means to you, you're less reliant on trying to find external certainties for comfort and reassurance.

The results of your efforts in the world are always uncertain. You can do all the right things and still not get what you want. But by determining your own meaning of success in the world, you can be certain of living a fulfilling life regardless of what happens externally. The third rule of chaotic happiness is founded on this premise. How you look at your world and the decisions you make have a substantial impact on your ability to find happiness.

THE THREE RULES OF CHAOTIC HAPPINESS

Now that you understand the three chaotic aspects of the world, you can start the process of overcoming them. The three rules I've designed for you to live by each target the chaos-producing aspects of the world. Happiness looks different for everyone, but what we all share is the need to address these challenging aspects of the world if we're to find the happiness we want for ourselves. Each of these rules is comprised of psychological exercises, thought experiments, and wellness strategies that will help you in your journey. Let's do a quick overview of each rule before diving into them over the next few chapters.

FIND YOURSELF

The first rule of chaotic happiness: Find yourself by developing self-awareness and building foundational self-esteem. Having a strong sense of self is the only way to make sure that the unavoidable stress and pressure of life don't break you. This process takes time and intentional effort, but as you work to understand yourself at a core level and build yourself up, you'll be less reliant on an uncharted world to guide you.

To do this work, you'll need to search yourself fully—leave no stone unturned. Knowing who you are and what you're made of is essential if you're going to overcome the disarray of an uncharted world. Specifically, you'll need to address beliefs about yourself that might be holding you back, and tackle internal obstacles that are blocking your path to being your fullest self. I'll provide the exercises to help you do this, but ultimately you need to be fully committed to this process if you want to find lasting success in this area.

By working wholeheartedly and making internal changes for the better, you'll be better able to confront the world's lack of direction. There may not be a map for life that shows you what path to take to be happy, but if you know who you are, then you have an internal compass to guide you. It's your internal strength and stability that makes you unshakable, even when the path forward isn't always clear or obvious.

For example, when you're being forced to take sides with friends or choosing between different work opportunities, finding yourself and your internal stability is your greatest asset. When there's no doubt inside you about who you are, it'll be easy to make a choice because you'll make one that fits the person you know yourself to be. Through the process of learning how to establish a solid sense of self, you'll discover what your core values are and what it means to uphold them with your actions. This will help making tough choices much easier, and you'll have a lot less regret because you'll know you made the decision that was right for you. That is what counts.

You'll also do a lot of work with inner change. You'll learn how to identify things you're holding onto internally, and then let those go to be fully yourself. A good example of something that prevents you from being yourself is inadvertently living for other people rather than for yourself, like when members of your family want you to act a certain way or friends encourage you to do things you normally wouldn't. You'll learn to see when you're swayed by others, and move away from this behavior. This will help you live the way you want, rather than living by someone else's expectations.

After doing the work to find yourself and living by this rule of chaotic happiness, you'll be someone whose sense of direction is driven by what you've established internally. You'll find more happiness in making choices based on the core beliefs you've discovered in yourself. This will help you overcome the anxiety of living in a world that doesn't give you clear directions on who you need to be and what you should be doing.

FIND YOUR PEOPLE

The second rule of chaotic happiness: Find the right people and maintain healthy relationships. This is key in creating the support system necessary for feeling secure in a world that is unpredictable. When we can count on the people around us, we're far more prepared to tackle the unexpected challenges presented to us head-on.

To live true to this rule, you'll need to learn how to evaluate the value of each of your relationships and practice setting boundaries. This is always easier in theory than it is in practice. It takes a lot of courage to cut someone out of your life who might not be good for you. It also takes a lot of courage to open yourself up to new connections who potentially could change your life significantly for the better. Regardless, when you practice the skills discussed in this book, you'll equip yourself with the ability to navigate your relationships in a new way—a way that will lead you to a place where the unpredictable is less scary because you know you have healthy relationships to lean on.

Another thing you'll work on is balancing your relationships. By establishing more equilibrium in your relationships, they'll be able to withstand more pressure. With the assurance that you have dependable relationships, there's less to be afraid of if something doesn't go according to plan. For instance, if you were to lose your job or experience loss, it's the comfort of having people there for you that helps to get you through.

When you learn to balance your friendships, you'll ensure your relationships are strong enough to lean on even with the added weight that accompanies unpredictable challenges.

The main point of this rule and its exercises is to help you find the right relationships and teach you how to maintain the ones you currently have. By mastering this rule, the unpredictable becomes less scary as you learn to find happiness by drawing it from a deep connection with others.

FIND YOUR PURPOSE

The third rule of chaotic happiness: Find your purpose by having a clear idea of your direction in life. Nothing is certain: That's the very definition of chaos. Knowing that all your work could ultimately result in failure anyway is an uncomfortable reality your have to live with. But when you have clear purpose in life, even when your efforts go unrewarded, you can take solace knowing that the meaning you've found for yourself behind every action is a reward of its own. When *you* decide the value of your actions and path, instead of circumstances deciding for you, you overcome the uncertainty of a world that can paralyze you.

To abide by this rule, you'll need to be able to look at the big picture and have clear direction despite all that is uncertain. You need to have meaning in your life. It can't be something that's easily shaken. You need to decide on a source of fulfillment for yourself that can't be taken away from you when it's put it to the test. The exercises provided will aid you as you search for a sense of purpose to help propel you to the next level. To go after what you want with everything you have requires the motivation that purpose provides and is an essential component for finding happiness.

Finding purpose holds particular value in uncertain situations, like when you don't know if the lessons you're teaching your kids are being internalized or when you don't know if all the work you're doing to study for a test will get you a better grade. When you focus on the purpose of your actions in the world more than on what happens in response to them, you find certainty in yourself rather than in the world. Feeling like you can rely on yourself instead of on the happenings of the outside world will bring happiness.

To find your purpose, something you'll be encouraged to work on is looking ahead. By developing your vision of what's to come and connecting it to your actions, you move away from judging yourself when you stumble. So when you, let's say, are trying to eat healthier or exercise more, you're going to misstep, and you have no guarantees of reaching the goals you set for yourself. But if you learn to value your effort and see the value in setting a goal for yourself in the first place, that will help you get through it. Learning to see the big picture means that uncertain results will have much less of a hold on you.

Learning and living by the rules of chaotic happiness gives us the toolset we need to combat the chaotic world we face every day. And don't worry if all of your tools aren't the sharpest when you first use them. This is a journey, and happiness is something you'll constantly have to work on. The good news is that there's always more happiness to be had. I think that's the best part. So, let's dig in, be patient, and work together to find chaotic happiness. I've seen people find it in the most unlikely of places and the most unlikely of situations. The difference between the people who find it and those who don't is courage. So let's be courageous and dedicate ourselves to finding happiness in ourselves, each other, and the world we live in.

RULE #1: FIND YOURSELF

If you're going to confront the chaos in the world in order to attain happiness, you first have to confront yourself. Through the process of systematically breaking down the parts of yourself that hold you back and building up the parts that make you resilient, you'll be better prepared to handle what life throws at you. And make no mistake, life will continue to challenge you in ways that you won't expect—in ways that attempt to break your spirit. However, by doing this work, you'll not only be able to meet the challenges, but you'll also be able to find a happiness that rises above them.

WHAT'S AT THE CORE?

This first piece of the puzzle is to find yourself, and in order to find yourself, you need to know yourself. When I say "know yourself," I'm not referring to what your favorite type of chips are or a pet peeve of yours. I'm talking about what's at the core of who you are as a person. What matters to you? What fills your cup? In the therapeutic process, this is always the first question I encourage my clients to explore. Let me walk you through an example.

I ask Michelle to tell me about herself. She starts crying; she recently got out of an abusive relationship and says she doesn't know how to answer that question anymore. It felt to her like her identity had been stolen. I spent the first few sessions working with Michelle on rediscovering her lost self.

It wasn't always this way for her. In fact, she'd show me pictures of her and her boyfriend and how happy they used to be. People are nuanced. They don't always show you who they are right away when you meet them. When Michelle met her boyfriend, her dream came true right before her eyes, until the dream slowly turned into a nightmare.

Gradually he became disillusioned with her. When he felt that he finally "had" her, she became an object to him. People are not objects, though, obviously, so he became frustrated that she didn't fit into his expectations of her. She was her own person, and this was never convenient for him. Gradually, though, he molded her into the character he wanted her to be, and she lost herself.

After a few weeks of therapy, Michelle was able to talk more and more about what she believes about herself at a core level. After a few months of work, she started to feel powerful again and more in control of her situation.

Often, the world is cruel like this, and we need to start again. I reminded Michelle that she had the courage to leave a bad situation and the courage to get help. We will start this process of recovery in much the same way. I'll outline how to get started in the next few paragraphs so you can begin your healing, rewarding journey.

With so much up in the air, your sense of self needs to be unshakable. To get there, you'll have to understand that being happy and feeling happy aren't the same thing. My hope for you is that you have the feeling of happiness often and feel it fully. However, feeling happy is not always going to be possible for a number of different reasons, primarily because the world is such a chaotic place. At any moment, something could happen to change your life forever. Accidents, illnesses, and traumas will inevitably happen, and they won't feel good at all. These cannot be prevented or prepared for. Life is going to hurt sometimes.

But even though life hurts, it's possible to be happy when it does. At the core of a fundamentally happy person is a solid sense of identity. Being happy internally consists of knowing who you are, knowing the person you want to become, and dedicating yourself to slowly moving toward that version of yourself, step by step, every day.

To get to this place of stability will require intention and an openness to challenge yourself. Before we begin the systematic process of breaking down the parts of you that you don't need anymore and helping you build yourself into the person you're trying to become, I need you to do some meaningful reflection.

EXERCISE: THE MIRACLE QUESTION

In a journal or on a piece of paper, write down the answer to the following question and put your whole heart into considering your response:

If a miracle happened overnight and suddenly you had the happiness you were hoping for, what would look different? What would you notice about yourself and how, specifically, would your life look different?

The miracle question is a tool that we as therapists use to help people explore what they have locked inside. The hopes and dreams people have stored away possibly haven't been considered in a long time because life gets in the way.

My guess is that after taking the time to think about it, you have a clearer picture of the person you're hoping to become than you previously realized. This will be important to your success and will assist you in the work to come. If the answer isn't yet clear, that's okay, too. Success in this process is ensured as long as you're willing to keep trying and exploring.

DIGGING DEEP

The next step on the path to happiness is digging deeper into the answer to your miracle question. In doing this, you'll find your core values, which shape how you see and interact with the world. You'll have to understand this aspect of yourself before you can start seeing yourself in a new way. You have to know what you value. If you don't, it will be hard to motivate yourself. If you do, you'll have confidence to take action, knowing why what you're working for matters to you.

Core values are something we learn in our childhood and continue to develop as we get older. Our values motivate everything we do, even if we don't consciously recognize them. The values that have the greatest impact on our actions are our *core* values. They're the ones that lie the deepest and were learned the earliest. The best way to illustrate how core values influence behavior is to think of the times in your life when you've been disappointed or proud of yourself. When you think about it, it's likely that your feelings of pride or disappointment in the past were closely linked to things you were taught to value. While values vary greatly from person to person, the values that people hold can generally be organized into a few different categories. In order to construct the version of yourself that can withstand the chaos, you'll need to understand who you are on the deepest level, right now, to be effective in your building. Let's start by discussing and exploring what your core values are.

EXERCISE: CORE VALUES

On the same piece of paper from the previous section, write down some things you don't want to live without. Think hard about this. Some examples: your pet, a hobby, vacations, children, or a certain career.

Let's explore some core values the things on your list might represent.

1. **CONNECTION:** If you've listed items like family, pets, or friends, you value connection and relationships. People with this core value often get their strength and motivation from caring for the people, pets, or even plants in their immediate environment. Quality of relationships may be a driving force for happiness.

2. **MASTERY:** If you've listed values such as excelling in academics, work, or a hobby, you value mastery—developing a high level of skill in something you enjoy. People with this core value experience happiness related to the power they feel when they've accomplished something they've worked hard on.

3. **ENJOYMENT:** If you've listed things like movies, parties, vacations, or sporting events, you value living life to the fullest in terms of enjoyment or fun. People with this core value experience more happiness when they can make the most of every moment.

4. **FREEDOM:** If you've listed situations like being in the moment, taking time for yourself, or enjoying the unexpected joys that life brings you, you value relaxation or freedom. People with this value often find happiness in being able to do what they want to do and going where the flow of life takes them.

These are just a few examples of common core values, and you may have other items not listed here, too.

What do these core values mean? Knowing your core values can point you toward areas in your life that need attention. If you find that one of these common core values is significant for you, you may need to pay more attention to how your current choices do or don't align with it. The chaos of life might be sidetracking you from the things that matter most. Being attuned to this can help you be intentional in making needed changes.

WHAT'S IN THE WAY?

How are you focusing on or ignoring your core values? How is external messaging getting in your way? What's missing in the equation?

Congruence. Congruence is the idea that true happiness is found when our actions and image of ourselves in the world match our deep-seated, internal core values. The importance of congruence was first discovered by psychologist Carl Rogers after his extensive research suggested that people with high levels of congruence typically also report having high levels of happiness. Living a congruent life is essential to true happiness, but in order to do that, you need to explore how exactly your external life and your core values might or might not be matching up.

> **CARL ROGERS'S** person-centered therapy is based on the idea that people inherently want to make positive changes in their lives. With the support of someone who provides unconditional positive regard and empathy (a therapist, for instance), people are better able to find happiness for themselves.

EXERCISE: LIVING CONGRUENTLY

Write down all of the things you do in a typical week. Both the ordinary things and the extraordinary things have a significant effect on your levels of happiness. Whether you're having a great day or just an okay one, how you're feeling depends largely on if what you're doing is congruent with what you value. A lot of unhappiness is caused by the mundane and repetitive parts of life. If you do the same boring or unpleasant things every day that have nothing to do with becoming the version of yourself that you want to be, that's a problem. It is essential to identify the big or small things incongruent to who you are that are draining your energy.

Compare this list of the things you do with the list you made in the last exercise. **In what ways do the things you do not match up with what you value most?**

CONNECTION

If you listed connection and closeness, what might be getting in the way of living out this core value? Often people who are experiencing difficulties with this aspect of life are struggling with boundaries and making choices about who to give their time to. If you're someone who puts a lot of stock into relationships, it might be difficult for you to say no to anyone. It might feel like a betrayal to your truest self to set limits with people at work or school. Because of this, you might be giving your energy to people in your life who may not deserve it—people who are demanding or critical—and neglecting the people who do—friends and family.

A problem that is also common with people who value connection is struggling with people-pleasing. People-pleasing consists of putting other people's needs first, all the time. While it may seem like being there for everyone would be congruent, it's actually incongruent. When you're constantly trying to please everyone, you're often spread too thin to make meaningful and deep connections with the people who matter the most.

MASTERY

If you listed building skills and mastery of your environment as a core value, frustration or lack of observable progress in doing the things you love might be inhibiting your happiness. If having control and a sense of accomplishment in your world is important, lacking those experiences drains your energy significantly.

You might also struggle with being given tasks and being told to develop skills that don't fulfill you, even if you have a natural talent for something. For instance, if you're a great singer and people notice, they may ask you to perform at events, do solos, learn specific songs, and so on, even if you don't want to develop this skill. Being forced or asked to do these things directly counters the values of control and accomplishment. (No hate toward parents, but this happens a lot when parents put pressure on their kids to do a certain hobby just because the kid is good at it.)

ENJOYMENT

If you listed living life to the fullest or enjoyment as a core value, struggling to find pleasure in certain activities and tasks that you have to do or that you're told to do gets in the way. The world will tell you that enjoyment is selfish and not a meaningful pursuit. The idea that activities need to be hard or exhausting in order to be meaningful is a common cultural message you might internalize that inhibits happiness.

Time management can also be a problem for people with this core value. It's far too easy to get caught up with the tasks you have to do rather than doing the things you want to do. When living life to its fullest, whether it's riding a roller coaster or going for a walk, getting sidetracked by other things that don't bring the same joy can put a significant damper on your happiness. Some days, you might find that you've spent all your time working at things that bring you no excitement or pleasure and you forgot to make time for the things that do.

FREEDOM

If you listed freedom as a core value, you might encounter the problem that spontaneity and relaxation are often interpreted as laziness or lack of productivity. You may internalize the messages that what you value most means you don't take life seriously enough or you aren't doing enough. This prevents you from living life in keeping with your core value of feeling free.

When you value freedom, you sometimes have a tendency to get bogged down with structure. You might have experienced this in school when a teacher gave an assignment with strict guidelines that left no room for you to approach it creatively, or at home if you have strict rules that boxed you in. When you're not allowed to be free, your creativity and openness to experience—your fuel—is stifled.

These are just a few of the things that might be affecting your ability to live congruently with your core values. The world is difficult enough, and if you're living incongruently with your own values, it's that much harder. Getting in your own way and doing things incongruently, things that don't give you fulfillment, greatly drains the energy you need to combat the chaos. Now that you have an understanding of what might not be lining up, we'll take a look at getting things realigned again in the next section.

CORRECTING DISTORTED VISION

When we begin the process of understanding our core self, we also find that at a core level, we're flawed. Some of the ways in which we view the world and the actions we undertake don't always line up. In fact, we all do this so frequently that it becomes a problem. Have you ever felt like you needed to get in better shape and then struggled to follow through at the gym? This is the kind of thing I'm talking about, but at a deeper level. Let me illustrate with another example.

Josh is in elementary school, and he's starting to get in trouble at school. His parents are bringing him to therapy because they think he's broken. No matter what they do, they can't get him to change his behavior, and they're worried that he's going to get expelled from school. They're doing the best they can and are desperate for a solution.

I meet with Josh and get to know him at a core level. On the outside, he's aggressive and reactive; he pushes people away. Usually this works for him, but not with me. When we keep digging, we get to who he really is. Josh is a kid who is having trouble at school because he wants to make friends but feels like he can't. Eventually, he says that he resorted to hitting other kids because they have been bullying him. However, this doesn't make sense because, after all, he's the one getting in trouble.

It turns out that at home, Josh has close relationships with his siblings. They all spend nearly all of their time together. As a result, a core belief of Josh's is that his relationships with his friends should resemble his relationships with his siblings. In reality, though, his core beliefs about relationships and the core beliefs of his peers are not the same. They're incongruent. These two things don't line up on a core level, and it is frustrating for Josh.

We had to correct Josh's view of ideal friendship with others to relieve that frustration.

Josh spent a lot of time thinking about how he could become more understanding of others and adjust his core beliefs in relation to his expectations. When working with Josh, I use superheroes as an example. What is the core belief of a superhero? Wanting to save the world. But when one superhero is working with another superhero, they need to understand that even though they're both trying to save the world, they won't do it in the same way. This is correcting and incongruence.

After a period of time working on this, Josh was able to adjust the way he values relationships relative to the realities of the world he lives in. He started making friends at school because he could understand that everyone is different from him in very fundamental ways.

You aren't seven years old, but if you develop the ability to correct and understand incongruence through the lens of your core values, you'll find the same balance that Josh did.

BLURRED VIEW

Do you sometimes criticize yourself for things your friends don't see? This is called a cognitive distortion, which is a fancy way of saying your view of yourself and the world is sometimes blurry. Having blurry vision when it comes to you and your world gets in the way of a happy life. It's like trying to walk down the sidewalk blindfolded. Most often, people develop blurry vision as a result of traumatic or difficult experiences. When you encounter a significant loss like losing a loved one or are hurt by people, your view of the world changes. The greater the pain, the greater the impact it has on your outlook. When you struggle to see the world objectively because you've experienced trauma, however small or large it is, it's challenging to be able to confidently live true to yourself because the open wound keeps festering. By understanding ways in which your outlook might be skewed, you'll be more aware of what inner healing may need to take place so you continue moving forward on the path to greater happiness. Let's take some time to explore some cognitive distortions that are common to each of the core values we previously discussed.

CONNECTION

If you value connection, the three cognitive distortions that most commonly skew your view are catastrophizing, emotional reasoning, and mind reading.

Catastrophizing is when you think the worst possible outcome is the most likely one in any given situation. If connection seekers have experienced something traumatic or difficult in one or more relationships, that leaves an imprint. You might struggle to seek or maintain the connection you need because you fear that what you experienced before will happen again.

Emotional reasoning means relying on the way you feel about a person or situation to interpret what happens, regardless of how likely your interpretation is. This might look like having a negative interaction with someone and convincing yourself it's your fault because you feel bad afterward. Feelings are subjective. They can be informative but are also often misleading.

Mind reading means you believe you can predict what a person will say or do without any evidence. When you attribute thoughts and feelings to people, you sometimes miss out on learning their true thoughts and feelings. This prevents connection. A friend might believe you're a fantastic friend, but you might interpret their unavailability to mean they don't value you. Learning how someone feels and thinks by interacting directly, rather than using your imagination, enriches your relationships.

AARON BECK, the founder of cognitive behavioral therapy, started studying cognitive distortions in the 1960s while treating people with depression.

MASTERY

People who value mastery tend to struggle with the cognitive distortions of personalization, shoulds, and overgeneralizing.

Personalization means taking personal responsibility for everything and everyone. When you value having control, you often end up taking on more than is good for you to handle on your own. You may be convinced you can do it all, but that comes at the expense of your own happiness.

Shoulds consist of setting unrealistic expectations about what you should do for yourself and other people. When you do this, you take on a lot of responsibility. Then you can't figure out what's realistic in the moment and focus on what you care most about. This is exhausting and leads to burnout.

Overgeneralizing means applying a message you receive in one area to all areas of your life. Say you're told you need to work harder to learn how to write a good paper. You then think you need to work harder in every area of your life and end up overexerting yourself. If you value control, you might struggle with this one. You like challenges, right? But taking on too much bogs you down.

ENJOYMENT

For people who value enjoyment, the most common cognitive distortions are ignoring positives, magnifying/minimizing, and fortune telling.

Ignoring positives consists of not being present for fun things. You might be out with a group of friends and feel sudden sadness. Your mind may drift off into something negative when at a family gathering. In the moment, you aren't experiencing the enjoyment you crave.

Magnifying/minimizing involves extra focus on minor things, such as something boring or a mistake you made, and less focus on achievements or pleasurable experiences. Fun seekers who do this struggle to prioritize their happiness compared with other things in their lives. You may also attribute more importance to work or school than is necessary because you've been told those are the most important parts of life.

Fortune telling consists of predicting something negative will happen, even if the prediction is unrealistic. People who value enjoyment are particularly affected by this. When you go into new experiences and "fortune tell" that it's going to go poorly, it makes it difficult to try new things. When your happiness is tied up in how well you're enjoying life, being held back by your fear of what might happen is a huge barrier.

FREEDOM

For people who value freedom, the most difficult cognitive distortions are all-or-nothing thinking, magical thinking, and jumping to conclusions. All of these cognitive distortions are related to feeling restricted.

All-or-nothing thinking is about seeing only two options for yourself: success or failure, right or wrong. There's no room for flexibility in this way of thinking. When you are too rigid in your thinking about things, there's no room to explore possibilities, which is what brings you the most happiness.

Magical thinking gives more power to thoughts and actions than is real. If you think one action will lead to finding romance and being happy, and it doesn't, then something must be wrong with you. This distortion gives an illusion of control. But if you're convinced a negative thought or mistake will ruin your life, you don't have much room to act and think in a creative, free way.

Jumping to conclusions means deciding what to do or think about something before knowing all the information. Freedom seekers tend to struggle with this one because they sometimes fail to be mindful that not every new thing will bring happiness. When enough things go wrong in seeking new opportunities, you might start to unconsciously assume that will always be the case. When freedom is important to you, you need to be able to remain open-minded, even when things are repeatedly not going your way. Jumping to conclusions directly impacts your ability to weigh options and be open to different ways of thinking and acting.

SEEING CLEARLY

So you have cognitive distortions, and you can identify what they are. What do you do about them so you can see the world clearly? Let's talk about some of the cognitive distortions mentioned and how to break them down so you can live more congruently.

1. Distortions associated with connection: Sometimes the best way to overcome the distortions associated with connection is to focus more on balance. It's unrealistic to expect yourself to not care a little too much for others or to always be able to prioritize your relationships. However, it is reasonable that you can consciously work on making more time for both so you don't miss out on what make makes you happiest.

2. Distortions associated with mastery: Control is definitely key here, and the best way to regain feelings of control is through accomplishment. The easiest thing you can do here is set small goals. By setting yourself up for success by tackling smaller challenges, you create a perpetual cycle of succeeding that will provide the needed momentum to make progress breaking down these distortions.

3. Distortions associated with enjoyment: The key with these distortions is learning to put yourself out there again, in whatever way that looks like for you. Relearning how to take stock of life and be grateful for what joy has to offer is often the best medicine. You need to remind yourself that fun is not a bad thing, and it's okay to seek it out.

4. Distortions associated with freedom: The most important thing to do when dealing with the distortions associated with freedom is to practice letting go. This seems like an obvious answer, but it's definitely not easy. The trick is repetition and learning to be comfortable with discomfort as you get accustomed to the feeling of lightening the load that's weighing you down.

EXERCISE: CHALLENGING COGNITIVE DISTORTIONS

Given what we've talked about regarding cognitive distortions, which ones do you think are affecting you the most, and what is your plan for working on them?

The key is to understand that distortions arise from negative or inaccurate thoughts. These thoughts get in the way of living congruently with your core values. By breaking down the distortions, you learn to think and feel differently about your experiences, make new choices, and see the world from a happier point of view.

BUILD A FOUNDATION

Knowing yourself and your various distortions leads into
the next part of the work you'll need to do to find yourself:
continue fine-tuning the changes you've made and
understand that process. You've formed some new habits and
new ways of thinking, but how do you maintain this change
and ensure that you can continue to make the proper
adjustments in new situations? Also, what will keep you
motivated in doing so? Having consistent motivation and
continuing to make insights is key to building the foundation
that will sustain them. Let's start with an example.

Todd has been in prison for the past six years. He stole a motorcycle when its owner ran into a gas station to get something to eat. Todd tried selling it to a dealership, but he was promptly turned in to authorities for possessing stolen property. While incarcerated, he had time to think about what he'd done. The person he used to be and the person he was after doing all of this internal processing were very different.

"What about now, though?" he asks me. "I'm tired of this, and I'm done with being stuck." The reason Todd asks this question is because this isn't his first time in therapy or his first time getting in trouble. Ever since he can remember, he's been stuck in the same cycle because he has been so strongly tethered to his addiction to substances. He'd done all of this internal processing before, but he always struggles to maintain it.

Todd needs to build a foundation that can support the work he's done and allow him to continue to do the work because there's so much left for him still to do. Todd's not leaving prison and headed straight to the country club; he's going back to being around the same people in the same environment. The work Todd and I are doing at this point is working to understand what challenges he'll face that he can change and what he cannot. For example, Todd can change whether he associates with people with active addiction, but he cannot change that as a convicted felon, he'll have a hard time finding high-paying jobs. Todd also needs to ensure that he can *stay motivated when his choice to stay clean becomes more challenging.*

Through our work together, Todd was able to develop a mindset that helped him maintain sobriety. He also identified his barriers. He changed what he could and found support systems to help him with what he couldn't. The more he did this, the more natural it became.

For the first time in a long time, Todd felt like he was standing on solid ground and maintaining internal changes. By doing these same things, you'll be able to find the same stability.

WHAT BLOCKS THE WAY?

Now you know at least some of your core values, and you understand what external messages and internal cognitive distortions make it harder to live congruently. It's time to figure out what in your life—people, situations, experiences, or conditions—are roadblocks to your happiness. Then you can use your strengths and motivations to create a path forward. This path has to be solid: a well-cleared trail through the woods, not a rickety bridge. Wouldn't it be great if you could just make internal changes to be happy? But the world presents obstacles. You need to know what you can change and what you can't.

So what's a roadblock? Something external—people, events, institutions, experiences—that either slows you down or stops you from following your path. There are two main types of roadblocks: movable and immovable. If you lose your wallet at home, that's a movable roadblock—you can look until you find it. If you develop a chronic illness, that's immovable—effort and action probably won't get rid of it.

But the key is not about identifying what is or isn't movable. It's learning how to find a way around something standing in your path to happiness if you can't move it. You have to problem solve. Remember, all-or-nothing thinking is a distortion, not reality. The goal is to think creatively to start seeing shades of gray.

EXERCISE: EXTERNAL OBSTACLES

Think of a particular obstacle you're dealing with right now. Look at your internal responses to the challenge.

- What's the obstacle?
- Is it movable or immovable?
- How has it affected your internal sense of peace?
- What core values is this obstacle challenging?
- What cognitive distortions may be making it more difficult to see clearly?
- What's one alternative (or more) to the way you're thinking about this obstacle based on that distortion?

This exercise helps you understand external constraints and challenges some of your cognitive distortions so you can find ways to move through or around the obstacle.

The next exercise focuses on your own agency. There's nothing more powerful than the words you use when talking yourself through your journey. You are your most important resource. Let's take a look at your inner script by exploring thoughts that don't serve you and how you can replace them.

WILLIAM MILLER and **STEPHEN ROLLNICK,** the founders of Motivational Interviewing, showed in research that the way in which a person talks to themself is an accurate predictor of the likelihood they end up making either positive or negative progress toward change.

EXERCISE: INNER SCRIPTS

Think about one of the obstacles in your life as you answer these questions.

- **What do you say to yourself about what you can't do?**
- **What thoughts do you have that drain your energy?**
- **Where do you seek external reinforcement?**

The first question is about limitations. Is there anything in the way you're talking to yourself that suggests you have a limited mindset? Thinking about what you can't do does nothing for you other than foster feelings of doubt and inadequacy.

The second question is about toxic thinking, which drains your energy. When you're out with friends, thinking about chores that aren't done or your midterm is not productive.

The last question is about the feedback that motivates you to keep making changes. If external validation is all you focus on, at some point you'll feel like you failed when you don't receive the validation.

Now go back to what you wrote above and answer these three corresponding questions:

- **What could you say to yourself instead?**
- **What thoughts give you energy and make getting out of bed easier?**
- **What do you want to hear from yourself when you accomplish something?**

You might have a problem that has to do with what's going on outside of you, and so you believe there is nothing you can do. Oftentimes this is true; problems like systemic oppression and wealth inequality won't be fixed solely by making internal changes. It's important to keep in mind that the purpose of making internal changes is not to solve problems, but to be better able to cope and adapt to them as they inevitably come. Mindfulness isn't about accepting or rejecting what the world brings us; it's about the power that lies in acknowledging what's there even if it's not changeable.

CREATE A PATH

Once you have a sense of what's in the way, you can start planning and finding your path. Easy, right? Not so much. You can have a great plan, but if you don't know how to create the conditions for it to happen, it won't. Choosing a destination is different from knowing how to get there.

A useful plan needs to encompass every aspect of you: your beliefs, the choices you make, the goals you set, and your developing self-awareness. If your goal is getting rid of anxiety and you hang around toxic people on the weekends, that will affect your progress.

When making your plan, it's helpful to structure it based on your strengths. Each skill is more or less important at any given time, depending on the obstacle you're facing.

MARTIN SELIGMAN founded the positive psychology movement. He identified that most research in the field was focused on what was going wrong with people rather than what was going right. He believes that finding and using your signature strengths is core to creating a happy life.

You're expecting a checklist of different strengths here, right? Nope. It would be a tragedy to limit what people are capable of to the things I could put on a list in this book. I won't let you off that easily.

If I gave you a list and you checked some boxes, would you believe those are your strengths, or would you try to convince yourself they are because I said so? Most of the time, it's the latter.

EXERCISE: FIND YOUR STRENGTHS

- Think about a couple of difficult things you've been through (but steer away from traumatic experiences that may trigger you right now). What qualities got you through these times?

- Now think about a couple of things you've accomplished. What qualities helped you succeed? What qualities did you develop as a result of these experiences?

You have already learned so much about building a good life through your past experiences. Use it to your advantage, and focus on the strengths you've identified. Every difficult thing you've been through is proof that you've found some way to survive. The incredible thing about building—or rebuilding—is that the approach you have is more important than the circumstances you face. This is the attitude I'm asking you to adopt.

FIND YOUR MOTIVATION

Using your past successes as a guide, it's time to start preparing for action. Happiness is a road trip, and you need gas to fuel your engine. Finding your motivation will keep you going as you make new choices and face new challenges.

How do you know that what motivates you now will still motivate you months or years from now? Well, there's no guarantee. People change, and so does what drives you. However, there are some fundamental motivations common to most people.

We don't know what changes will happen, but we can know what will likely be consistent. When we conceptualize motivation, we often think about basic life tasks or goals we'd like to accomplish. Your happiness may depend on your ability to achieve them. The three tasks I'm about to explain can provide a framework for thinking about your own motivations.

Alfred Adler was a psychiatrist who worked alongside Freud and eventually formed his own school of thought. An essential aspect of Adlerian Theory is that people are goal-oriented. In working toward a happy life, people strive to complete three basic life tasks: work, friendship, and love.

The first life task has to do with friendship and belonging, or feeling like you have a place in the world. This can mean a variety of things. It could be feeling at home in a mountain cabin or being the CEO of a large company. The collective theme of this task, however you complete it, is feeling that you have a place where you fit in. While this may seem like a simple idea, if you take the time to reflect, when you don't feel like you belong, there's much less happiness to be had.

The second universal life task has to with finding a calling and purpose, or having something you love to do and feeling like doing it matters. There's an endless number of things that could fulfill this task. Contrary to popular belief, there's no such thing as a meaningless activity or something not worth doing. Whether you fulfill the task is not defined by the choice of activity itself. What matters is the collective theme, which is loving what you do and finding a way to do it well.

The third universal life task has to do with love and intimacy, or connecting with people and forming meaningful relationships. To be able to feel happy, it's important for you to feel like you've made a lasting impression on others. Sometimes this is through what you achieve, and oftentimes it's through the people you meet. While love and connection are accomplished differently by different people, the core is that we all need to feel we have left a legacy.

It's important to understand universal life tasks because they're behind most of what motivates you. We all share these needs in some way, shape, or form. Now would be a good time to reflect on how you fulfill the universal life tasks for yourself.

EXERCISE: REFLECTING ON LIFE TASKS

1. Draw three columns on a piece of paper, one for each life task, and write the things in your life that fulfill each of them for you.

2. Look at each column. What area isn't getting enough attention?

3. Which areas are you doing well in?

The purpose of taking the time to reflect on where you're at in completing the universal life tasks is to gain perspective. Sometimes, knowing how you're doing in the grand scheme of things gets neglected because you're so caught up in the day to day. When you know what you want, how to adjust your perspective, and how to see the big picture, you're ready to start the process of real change.

THE STAGES OF CHANGE

Progress can be deceptive. You might feel like you're doing really well and then a week or two later like you're back to square one. On the surface, there's not much difference between someone who's made meaningful change and someone who's made change because they mean to go home. I see this a lot as a therapist. People make significant changes in their appearance, diet, or activity, and it's not always enough. While changing things on the surface can be impactful, deeper change needs to go along with it.

To figure out where you are in making meaningful progress, it can be helpful to think about stages of change. There are five stages:

1. **PRECONTEMPLATION:** You haven't started thinking about making a change. Maybe it hasn't been a priority, or you have been distracted by making friends or trying to find a decent job.
2. **CONTEMPLATION:** You're considering making changes and clarifying your thoughts (values, cognitive distortions, and internal scripts). By this point in the book, you've given thought to the changes you're seeking.
3. **PREPARATION:** You're making plans. You're doing this by working through this book. Change is not always a linear process—you might be in preparation for a change and then move back into contemplation.

4. **ACTION:** You're taking action based on your preparation. This part of the journey is the most perilous and also the most rewarding. This might be where you're stuck right now.

5. **MAINTENANCE:** You may have succeeded in your intentions and arrived at your goals. More than that, you're growing into the person you want to be and feeling the benefit of your efforts.

> Two psychologists, **JAMES PROCHASKA** and **CARLO DICLEMENTE,** created the stages of change in the 1970s based on their studies of smokers who were able to quit on their own compared to those who needed treatment to do so.

Knowing where you are in the process of change can provide insight into what you might need to push yourself to the next level. As you progress through the stages of change, it will be increasingly important to check in with yourself as you move along. This prevents you from burning out and overextending yourself by moving too fast.

Remember that change is not a linear process. But when you've fallen in love with the process, your progress, and your purpose, you will have the energy to keep going.

KEEP FAILING TO SUCCEED

You've learned all the tools you'll need to become a happier person who really knows yourself, but becoming the best version of yourself is a hard journey. You will fail, more than once, before you get where you want to go. That's okay— failing is part of the process.

You can do all the internal work to understand yourself, resolve your incongruencies, and find a structure to help keep you motivated in making changes but still fail miserably sometimes. You're going to fail, whether it's as a result of your actions or not, and it's going to hurt. The greater the ambition in the change you make, the harder the fall if you fail. And make no mistake, you are making some ambitious, fundamental changes in working through the first rule of chaotic happiness. To understand how to deeply learn from your failure, and how to keep trying, is an important part of this process.

Jake and I have been working together for some time now. He was struggling with feelings of depression a year ago but was doing better recently. He did all the internal work and created structures for himself to maintain change. However, Jake's body recently rejected the kidney transplant he got. Jake is shutting down at home, he's not talking to anyone, and he barely eats anything.

Jake and I spent our time together at this point just talking about the hurt of experiencing failure through no fault of his own. This is crucial because we'll always experience failure like this from time to time, that doesn't need to or can't be fixed, but rather must be felt and understood. Learning to cope with failure, yours or the failure caused by living in the imperfect world we live in, gives you the necessary peace to keep trying.

Eventually, Jake did get another transplant, and we focused not only on the victory, but also on his courage in continuing to try to be healthy.

Your situation may or may not be like Jake's. You might be trying to make a change like being more organized, and then you keep getting distracted. The same principle holds true, though, and that's what we'll focus on. Whether your failures are life-altering or less so, how you approach them makes all the difference in being able to be happy despite all the unavoidable chaos.

FAILING

Successful people are world-class in failing. I wish I could tell you it was as easy as brushing yourself off and getting back up, but there's heartache involved in failing, especially when you're trying to make core changes. However, there's a difference between heartbreak and heartache. The first holds you back, while the second helps you continue to grow.

One aspect of a failure that leads to heartbreak is self-punishment. If you make a mistake and don't reach a goal, and you start criticizing yourself, that's a warning sign. Psychologically speaking, punishment is a terrible motivator. It creates stress, which actually affects your brain structure so it's less able to function and adapt. Punishment might be useful in discouraging bad behavior, but it does nothing to build good habits.

> Research isn't commonly done on punishment because there's no way to ethically carry it out. Our understanding of the effects of punishment has largely evolved from research done regarding trauma. Induced stress, of which punishment is a significant form, correlates heavily with health problems and decreased prefrontal lobe functioning, the part of the brain responsible for critical thinking.

Better to learn from the heartache of a failure. You can sit with the pain of your failure for the purpose of learning from it. The key thing is that when you're learning from the heartache, don't sit in it a second longer than the time you need to learn its lessons. When something hurts and thinking about it runs you around in circles, that's a pretty good indicator that it might be time to do what you can to move forward.

Something that can also lead to heartbreak is trying to spin the failure into something positive—finding the silver lining. This is probably not what you've heard before, so let me explain. Trying to see an experience as something it *objectively* wasn't is not healthy. You can't think your way out of the pain of the experience. That's just denial, and denying the truth leads to a cycle of being stuck.

Rather, let yourself experience heartache and find meaning in failure. This requires introspection and is completely within your control. It's an exercise in taking back power and finding purpose when you're at your lowest. In making the decision to grow when something else is tearing you down, you demonstrate and foster the courage you'll need to be happy whenever times get tough.

The most heartbreaking part of failure is seeing it as permanent. This is perhaps the most common reason people don't become who they want to be. You may get stuck in this idea because you get wrapped up in the negative feelings of the moment or have a closed mindset. When you fail, you might need to rethink your plans or adjust a goal, but failure never means your life is unalterable.

The alternative is to be open-minded and see failure as an opportunity—an opportunity to learn something about yourself, seek out a new skill, or take a closer look at your goals. If you can remember that there's always possibility, you can continue to grow. Failure is the key to success. Here are a few questions to spark reflection on failure.

EXERCISE: A LESSON IN FAILURE

For this exercise, pick a failure in your life that you've been trying to work through recently but have had a hard time with. Ask yourself the following questions:

Is it your fault?

   A. If yes, did you do it on purpose?

   B. If you also answered yes to this, did you do it intentionally to hurt someone?

   C. If you answered yes to this as well, are you feeling guilty or remorseful?

   D. If it's not your fault, then what is it that is preventing you from moving forward? Write a few sentences hypothesizing what might be going on and things you can keep working on to help you push through.

Regardless of who you are, if you're having a hard time working through something, it's because you're human—human in the sense that everyone is flawed on many levels, and even if something's not our fault, we feel it is. When you make a mistake, you're likely the last one to forgive yourself. Sometimes all it takes is asking yourself a simple set of questions like these as a reminder to treat yourself better or practice being better rather than focusing on your hurt.

TRYING AGAIN

So you've experienced failure. Now it's time to apply what it's taught you. To do this, get good at looking for the next opportunity. Opportunity isn't always obvious. What does opportunity look like, and how can you be sure not to miss it? When should you keep trying, and when is it time to call it quits? Answering these questions helps you make sure you're putting your energy into things that move you closer to what you hope to achieve.

EXERCISE: LEARNING TO REASSESS

Take out your journal and answer the following questions about what you're currently working on. Keep these in mind as you figure out your next opportunity.

What do I plan to learn? An important part of growing is learning, and true opportunity should always include being able to learn something. If you don't think you can learn anything new in what you want to try, it may be time to move on to something else.

What progress can I make? Anything worth your effort will bring you closer to your goals. If something doesn't provide forward momentum, it might not be worth doing.

What purpose does it serve? This is about meaning. Does the next thing you want to try align with your core values or your vision for your future? If it doesn't, find something that does. When you've decided an opportunity is worth your energy, remember to apply the lessons you learned from previous failure.

Constantly trying is the key to success. We'll talk about it more in the next section. The point is that when you're trying something again, you need to make sure your energy is not wasted in the wrong places.

SUCCEEDING

When will you know you've arrived? Just engaging in the process is arriving, and you're already doing that. To live a happy life in a chaotic world, you have to constantly become a better version of yourself. This may seem like a tall order to fill, but I'm certain you can do it. There are a lot of things you can do to ensure continued growth. Sometimes it's setting big goals for yourself, and sometimes it's learning a new skill like self-compassion. The key thing is not to become static. If you're not progressing, you're regressing. There's nothing sadder than becoming happy for a little while and then watching it fade away. The good news is that there's no reason your growth needs to diminish in that way.

The bottom line is that you determine what it means, not anyone else. There's no such thing as failure as long as you continue to try; as long as you're giving it everything you've got. This seems like a simple idea, but it's so easy to forget because the world puts so much pressure on us. You need to make a promise to yourself that your happiness and growth are your first priority.

EXERCISE: MAKING A PROMISE TO YOURSELF

Making a promise to yourself is a great way to work on who you want to be. By making a contract with yourself, you're setting a clear standard for yourself and what succeeding means to you, while also holding yourself accountable. I call this setting a contract rather than a goal because it's all about a willingness to engage in the process of change, not trying to get to a destination.

The questions below are a guideline, but write your contract any way you want. You're answering to yourself, not to me.

- What are your core values?
- What cognitive distortions do you sometimes struggle with?
- How have you addressed these so far, and what do you plan on addressing in the near future?
- What external obstacles are you facing?
- What can be changed and what can't?
- How will you keep making progress toward your goal?
- What will be your signs of success and of failure?
- What is your plan to keep growing?

Spend as much time with this exercise as it takes to feel proud of your contract. Do whatever it takes to internalize it. Read through this chapter several times if you need to. Finding yourself is just the first phase in your journey.

CHAPTER LEARNINGS

- Understanding your core values gives you insight into what motivates your choices and why you feel the way you do.
- Unhappiness has to do with the absence of feelings and actions that line up with your core values.
- Congruence is living in accordance with your core values and is an essential aspect of a happy life.
- Cognitive distortions are ways of seeing the world and yourself inaccurately, usually based on past negative experiences.
- You can increase your happiness by learning how to identify and challenge those distortions.
- Looking closely at internal and external obstacles can help you figure out how to work around them.
- Use your strengths and past successes to help figure out how to meet the roadblocks in your life.
- Find your own motivations to help create a plan for a happier life.
- Failing is an inevitable part of the growth process. Learn from failure and try again.
- Commitment to yourself is the most important factor for finding long-term success.

RULE #2: FIND YOUR PEOPLE

You can work on yourself as much as you want, but you need other people, too. In order to weather life's uncertainty, you'll need to build a strong network of people who support you and who you support in return. While it may be cheesy, there's a lot of truth in the saying "True wealth is measured by the quality of your relationships." Finding the right people and fostering healthy relationships not only brings comfort, but it also pushes you to the next level. The wealthiest and most successful people in the world are often the first to point out the people behind the scenes who helped to get them where they are today. You'll need to find the same type of people who will help you in your journey to achieve happiness in the midst of the difficulties the world sometimes brings.

WHO WEIGHS YOU DOWN AND WHO LIGHTENS THE LOAD?

When you start to see your own path to happiness, it's important to understand how the people around you fit into the journey. You need people in your life you can count on. How are the relationships you already have? Some, I'm sure, are good, and some are . . . well, something else.

The second thing we'll be working on, and the second rule for chaotic happiness, is finding your people. Finding your people is essentially just finding the *right* people—people who you feel you connect to at a core level, like what we talked about in rule #1. Having these solid relationships is essential to happiness. Relationships can cause you to feel burdened and weighed down, or they can help you feel light and worry-free. Understanding the impact the people closest to you have on your happiness is key in fostering the relationships you'll need to find happiness. Here's an example.

Sarah does everything for everyone. When she told her parents she wanted to see a therapist, they almost didn't believe her. She's a perfect example of an overachiever and excels in every area of her life. She participates in debate team, gymnastics, a church group, volunteer work, and so on; if I listed them all, it would be a very long list.

Sarah hates it when her parents and other people in her life act like she's invincible. She's so good at putting on a brave face that people rarely bother to ask her how she's doing because they don't see anything wrong. In fact, others ask Sarah to do more than anyone else because "she's so reliable and we can count on her to follow through." No one knows that she's drowning.

It turns out Sarah sought out therapy because she hadn't been eating. The pressure Sarah put on herself to perform at a high level in gymnastics had caused her eating patterns to become dysregulated. She felt it necessary to be at an "ideal weight" and started eating irregularly. This greatly affected her appetite, even when the season was over, and she sought my help.

We spent the summer working through the concepts and exercises in rule #1, and things got better. She understood herself more, who she was at a deep level, and rid herself of the cognitive distortions contributing to her disordered eating habits. But when school started, her problem returned.

Sarah's relationships, who she was surrounded by and how they interacted with her, were having just as much of an impact on what she was experiencing as her inner self was. What we worked on at this point was learning how to assess relationships in order to be aware of their impact. In doing this work, Sarah was able to connect the dots to how the people in her life were holding her back, and how they made her feel, were affecting both her happiness and her health.

The way we talk about relationships in psychology is through systems theory. The idea is that each relationship in your life is like a system of many different moving parts. Each system you're in (your family is a system, your romantic relationship is a system, you and your best friend are a system) has different rules that dictate how each part works together. So, when we're looking to understand the health or dysfunction of a system, we're looking at how these rules influence communication patterns and dynamics that exist between each person in the system. If one person or part of the system is not functioning properly, most likely there are systemic issues at play creating or influencing the problem rather than just the individual person themself.

So, let's talk about your relationship systems. If something isn't working, it's a combination of what you're bringing to the relationship and what the other person is. The next few exercises will help you evaluate your relationships. Are they functioning the way you want them to? Is the system one that creates conflict for you? Most important, will the system help you get where you want to go, or not?

Let's start this exploration with your current relationships to find out what might be holding you back and what relationship opportunities will support your happiness.

WHO WEIGHS YOU DOWN?

Consider the purpose of relationships with friends, family, partners, and acquaintances. Relationships are about connecting with other people for mutual benefit. Every person in your life should contribute to you becoming your best self (and vice versa), but it's rare that this is the case. Sometimes we feel obligated to show up for people who don't do the same for us. If most of your relationships are like this, they will weigh down your journey toward growing into the happiest version of yourself.

EXERCISE: WHO WEIGHS YOU DOWN?

Grab your notebook and draw a balance scale.

- Identify a relationship in your life that feels hard.
- On one side of the scale, write what they do for you.
- On the other side, write what you do for them.

Now do an assessment. Is there a clear imbalance? Which side is heavier? Keep in mind that what you "do" for someone or what they "do" for you doesn't have to be an action. The smile of someone you love or the kindness in their eyes is as meaningful as anything else.

Repeat this exercise for as many relationships as you want, especially ones you may feel confused about. It will give you clarity.

MURRAY BOWEN was the first psychologist to apply systems theory to family therapy. When working to address one person's distress, he looked at was happening in the person's relationships.

One of the most frequent mistakes people make in relationships is holding double standards—specifically, having unrealistically high expectations of yourself and low expectations of others. Sometimes you move mountains for other people's happiness but don't expect the same thing in return. When you care about someone, your first instinct is to give more than you get; this is beautiful. But sometimes giving too much impacts not only your own health, but also the health of the relationship and the other person(s). A good example is family members, partners, or friends who make the same mistake repeatedly while continually coming to you for help or forgiveness when it happens. You find yourself disappointed and hurt when this cycle keeps repeating. Your help might not actually be truly helping, and you're sacrificing your own happiness in the process.

Such double standards are what weigh us down. We often give far more that we get from others. We tell ourselves we need to accept whatever they give us. But if your goal is to find happiness in the chaos, you'll need to change this relationship dynamic. You're not a superperson. You can't do everything for everyone and have enough left in the tank to care for yourself.

There will be times when your relationships aren't balanced, and that's okay. Sometimes we do more for others and sometimes they do more for us. *Chronic* relationship imbalance is what I'm suggesting you address. One of the most difficult parts of relationships is recognizing when you've outgrown one. Letting go of any kind of close relationship is not easy.

WHO LIGHTENS THE LOAD?

It's just as important to recognize the relationships in your life that are lightening the load. What are characteristics of the relationships that make your life easier and more joyful? Pinpointing which relationship dynamics contribute to your growth is important—it helps build awareness of what to look for when assessing the value of current and future relationships.

EXERCISE: WHO LIGHTENS THE LOAD?

Write down the names of about five people in your life. (Having multiple examples increases the effectiveness of the exercise.)

- How do these people make your life better? Write down three to five qualities.
- Now compare each list. Are there any qualities that stick out to you or characteristics they have in common? Try to pick out three.

Analyze why the three qualities you chose have such a positive impact on your life. Which people embody those qualities? What about these people helps you feel stronger, happier, and more confident?

Seeing the aspects of relationships that build you up will allow you to better understand not only the type of people you want to be around, but also the type of person you are.

A key part of friendship is sharing core values. It's likely that the strengths your friends have complement your own strengths. It's true that on the surface, healthy relationships often consist of people who are very different from each other with interests and skills just as diverse. This is good because having relationships with people who are good at what you're not, and vice versa, creates an atmosphere of mutual learning and growth. Naturally, just by being around a person with a different strength, you sharpen that strength for yourself.

But on a deeper level, the important thing is that your core values align. You can do different things and have different interests, but it's essential to have a common purpose. The different avenues and paths you take to live out your core values amongst your group doesn't matter. What matters most is that, in whatever road you take, you work cohesively with the people around you and agree on what you think the important things are in life. If someone around you deeply values something you don't, you won't be effective in encouraging them to live true to it, and vice versa. Find people who are incredibly different from you, but who at the end of the day find meaning in the same things you do.

CLOSING AND OPENING DOORS

Once you start to learn more about how your relationships affect your happiness, the question becomes what you should do with this information. Sometimes it's necessary to close the door on some of your relationships for the sake of your happiness. Likewise, you'll also sometimes need to open the door for new or deeper relationships. You only have room for these relationships that bring you closer to who you want to be. Let me walk you through an example of what this process looks like.

Stacy is a college graduate student, and she's struggling to balance the two most important relationships in her life: with her father and with her partner. Her father has been difficult to connect with in the past couple of years since she came out of the closet after many years of hiding her queer identity from him.

In recounting the story, she describes that he didn't react angrily but asked her if she was sure or maybe confused. She wasn't surprised by his ignorance, and she was glad he did not angrily reject her. What was shocking to her was how much his tolerance hurt her. "To be tolerated hurts me. I want to be accepted, not have my identity put up with like an inconvenience."

Stacy loves her dad, and ever since her mom passed away when Stacy was 14, they've been inseparable. From that point on, all they had was each other's support. Whenever she was dealing with something, he was the first person she'd call. There's not been a day in her life where she says she didn't feel loved by him.

Now, though, while she knows her father still loves her, their relationship is different. She says, "When I'm around him, he looks at me like I'm somebody else, like the version of me he felt he could relate to died when I told him I was a lesbian." She had hoped that in the two years since she had told him that his ignorance would fade and things would be the way they used to be.

Aside from her dad, the other important relationship in Stacy's life is with her partner, Kris. After coming out of the closet, Stacy finally had the confidence to put herself out there more in public. In came Kris. They met at the library on campus and laughed at being "the only old people" there. Stacy says, "When I'm with Kris, I feel safe and loved."

The problem is that Stacy's dad refuses to meet Kris. Kris is becoming more and more frustrated that Stacy will spend the holidays with her father while she's left flying solo, explaining to her parents the existence of her mysterious partner, Stacy, whom they've never been able to meet. But Stacy knows she's all her father has and doesn't want him to spend the holidays alone. At the same time, the holidays feel so much emptier without Kris.

In therapy, Stacy had already done the work to understand her relationships. Now she needed a plan for improving them. She spent time deciding which doors to close and which to open in these relationships in order to be happy. She chose to close a door to aspects of her relationship with her dad in order to open more doors in her relationship with Kris.

To identify the aspects that needed to be let go of, we used the following exercises as a guide.

WHEN TO CLOSE DOORS

Being able to identify the health of your relationships is one thing. Actually making change, however, is entirely another. We might have a solid idea about which relationships are positive and which aren't, but it can still be hard to figure out when to end one and when to work on the relationship more. Knowing how to do this is a skill. It requires both self-awareness and the courage to take action. So when do you need to cut someone out of your life for the sake of your own happiness? The only person who will know this for sure is you. What are you willing to allow in your relationships?

Everyone reading this book will have a different answer. For instance, if working to preserve the planet through action is an important core value for you and your friend doesn't share this value, you might choose to close a door. For another person, caring for the environment may be important, but not enough to end relationships over. There's no one answer.

The main consideration here is how each relationship you have does or doesn't contribute to you to being your happiest self. If there's a relationship in your life that is not helping you be the person you want to be, it may be worth it to consider closing the door to it partially or fully.

In the last section, you put thought into the quality of your relationships, so now you can consider the steps to closing a door on a relationship that weighs you down: expecting, engaging, and executing.

1. **EXPECTING:** First, think about what you want from the other person. This is called setting expectations. Does taking space mean zero contact, or does it mean you want to spend less time together? Giving someone clear expectations does two important things: First, it lets them know what they will need to do to respect your boundaries, and second, it helps to create a new dynamic in the relationship.

2. **ENGAGING:** Prepare for the expectation-setting conversation. Where and when will you have it? Consider if you want to do it in person or virtually. Think about the expected response. If someone has aggressive tendencies, for instance, it might make sense to have a conversation in a public setting.

3. **EXECUTING:** The last part of the process is following through. It's just as important for you to follow the expectations you've set as it is for the other person to do so, especially when closing the door on someone who might have toxic tendencies. The best way to make sure you get the change you want is to hold your own boundaries.

EXERCISE: CREATING DISTANCE

Think of a relationship you've identified that is draining or simply not supporting you in being your best self, and consider each of the three steps for closing the door.

1. Expecting: Write down the first couple of sentences you will say to this person when having the conversation about closing the door.

2. Engaging: Write down two expectations you have around the shift in your relationship.

3. Executing: Imagine a scenario in which the person doesn't respect one of those boundaries and what you will say in response.

Don't go into these conversations without planning first. They're hard to have. If the person you're trying to remove from your life gets pushy, you might find yourself caving if you don't know quite how to respond.

WHEN TO KEEP DOORS OPEN

Being more open carries with it a different kind of fear than deciding to close a door. It's vulnerability that sometimes leads to unhappiness in the first place. The times you've been hurt the most probably started with giving another person the chance to get close to you.

If vulnerability involves so much risk, why do it? Even though vulnerability sometimes leads to pain, it's worth the risk because it also can lead to connections that bring us the greatest joy. The people who surround us significantly affect our happiness. Taking chances to make connections with people who could support you in your journey is worth it.

There are a few characteristics to look for in people who can help you on your path to happiness.

The first is authenticity. Someone who is comfortable being themself is not likely to be a burden. In fact, someone living authentically is likely to also be on a path to happiness. This person has found a way to accept their unique qualities. We often try to fit in; authentic people don't mind sticking out. When we're able to move past the notion of who we "ought" to be, we are free to pursue what truly makes us happy.

You'll want the people with whom you choose to be open to be nonjudgmental. Imagine that your happiness is a plant. Judgment is a cloud that blocks the sun and withers the plant. When a person is critical, it's harder to grow into your new life. Have you ever had a friend who was in a bad relationship with another person that changed them? Sometimes you can even evaluate photos of someone before and after being in the relationship; they might look entirely different. Judgment and criticism break you down, and being in a relationship where that's constant takes a toll. Constant judgment serves to cut off the supply of sun that you need for happiness.

On the other hand, when people in your life encourage you, it helps you reach new heights. The first thing people usually do when they win a prestigious award is say thank you. It's because they know that achieving their dreams became a reality because of the encouragement they received from other people along the way. Encouragement is just like criticism, but it's incredibly constructive rather than destructive. With enough of it in your life, it helps you achieve the happiness you're aiming for, and also the happiness others pushed you toward that maybe you didn't see yourself.

Lastly, people you foster relationships with should possess empathy. If someone can't imagine being in your shoes, they won't have a lot to offer in helping you take your next steps. People who are able to see life from your perspective can give validation when things are tough, offer insight when you're struggling with a choice, and celebrate with you when things are going well. Empathetic friends help you feel less alone in the journey toward happiness.

EXERCISE: KEEPING DOORS OPEN

- Imagine feeling accepted just as you are. Who gives you that feeling?
- Imagine feeling supported. Who do you feel that around?
- Imagine feeling encouraged to be yourself. Who provides this encouragement?

People possess many characteristics that serve to make another's life better. The purpose of this exercise is to help you identify which of these characteristics impact you the most. Finding something you've never had requires stepping through doors you've never been through. Having the right support system can give you the confidence to keep taking those nerve-wracking steps into the unknown in your pursuit of happiness.

BLOCK THE WAY OR CLEAR THE PATH?

Reassessing boundaries is crucial for continued success in relationships. People change over time, and so will the elements that are best for the relationship (and for you). While sometimes your next step will be obvious, it's often not.

Let's determine the potential effects of choosing to either close a door or leave it open. It can be hard to figure this out in the abstract, so this exercise will make this choice more concrete. Choosing to shut someone out of your life or open yourself up to another takes courage. Clarify your reasons ahead of time to make it a whole lot easier.

EXERCISE: RELATIONSHIP INVESTMENT

Think of a relationship in which the best next step for you is not clear.

Imagine you decide to close the door.

1. **Write two lists. What would you lose? What would you gain?**
2. **Give the items on each list a value from $1 to $10 based on how important they feel to you. Add them up.**
3. **What's the net cost or profit of this choice?**

Now do the same for keeping the door open. Which choice costs more?

Use this process to consider other relationships in your life. Are there any costing you a lot with very little reward? It may be time to close that door. Are there any relationships you're hesitant about but that have potential to pay dividends? In this case, consider allowing yourself to be more vulnerable with those people. Sometimes when someone we're close with, such as a family member, takes more than they give, it can end up costing too much. Consider places to reinvest the energy, such as with people at work who have the potential to offer new opportunities.

ASSERTING BOUNDARIES

What you need most when closing and opening doors is the ability to be assertive. Assertiveness is an approach to communication that focuses on balancing being supportive of others and your own self-respect. By being assertive, you ensure that you'll not only be able to maintain your own happiness, but also protect it from the various chaotic things that sometimes try to get in the way (such as other people putting their problems on you, etc.).

In *The Assertiveness Workbook*, clinical psychologist **RANDY PATERSON** explains that assertiveness is about being genuinely present in the relationship, allowing yourself to share your wants and needs, and inviting the other to share their wants and needs, as well.

Understanding your relationships and knowing what needs to be changed is important, but all this work means nothing if you can't execute these things. The best and most balanced way to make the relationship changes that you've identified for yourself is through assertiveness. Assertiveness, which will be reiterated later in the chapter, is using clear, concise, and direct communication. One of the most important ways to be assertive and what we'll be working on is asserting the boundaries (closed door/open door) that you've decided on for your relationships. Here's an example.

> *Jeff knows what needs to change in his relationship with his mom, and he knows the impact it's having on his happiness. However, Jeff struggles to set boundaries with her. He says that "she's super invasive and has no sense of privacy." He recognizes that she's lonely (being a widow), and that she has little else to concern herself with other than him. But it's starting seriously to take a toll on him, constantly having her in his business. So far, he's been ineffective in setting boundaries, and it's affecting multiple areas of his life.*

Jeff works at a local bank as a loan officer and is married with no children. His mom constantly brings up in conversations with his wife when she's going to have a baby. Jeff has requested his mother not do this, but she doesn't listen and then eventually does it again.

When Jeff is at work, his mom will come visit with the bank tellers during his work hours. Sometimes she brings a lunch for the two of them to share. He says she's been like this for years, and "her insane antics are literally making me crazy." She constantly calls him, and he decided to come to therapy to process his stress and find a solution.

During our sessions, Jeff practiced reflecting on his situation and building up his communication to be more assertive. Outside of sessions, Jeff was able to establish boundaries and make the relationship changes he outlined for himself through his assertiveness skills.

After a lot of practice, Jeff learned to be more direct and clear in communicating with his mom. You can do this, too. Here are some things to help get you started.

SAYING NO

If you're too passive in communicating a new boundary, your message may not be clear enough for the other person to take it seriously or to even understand it. On the other side, if you're too aggressive, this can create more conflict in your life. Instead of simply hearing and respecting the boundary, someone might get defensive or try to argue with you about it. The middle ground of assertiveness lies between being passive and being aggressive. To assertively close a door, you'll want to be mindful of different aspects of communication that have the greatest effect: body language, word choice, and tone.

Body language is as simple as it sounds—it's what you convey based on how you carry yourself. The best way to communicate assertiveness with your body is to maintain good posture, keep your shoulders back and relaxed, and make appropriate eye contact. By carrying yourself this way, you embody the message you're trying to get across: that you're confident in your choice.

The words you choose are significant. When closing a door, your words should reinforce the boundaries you're setting. Words and phrases such as "I think," "maybe," "could be," and "for now" can imply a temporary boundary or that you aren't sure about what you're saying. Compare these two sentences:

- I think we're spending too much time together and maybe we should change that.

- I'm feeling overextended and need to spend less time with you.

Which one communicates a clear boundary? If your words line up well with your mission, you'll be more successful in establishing distance.

Tone, timing, and inflection are also crucial parts of being assertive. Seemingly tiny differences in how you speak can have a big impact, and you can use that to your advantage. For example, say you're stepping back from a friendship with someone who betrayed your trust. Letting your hurt show in your voice communicates why you need to close the door. People respond to emotion more strongly than to information, and you can use your tone and inflection to make that emotion clear.

We're taught to say yes to things (like more work or a party invitation) but not to say no. So let's practice.

EXERCISE: HOW TO SAY NO

Imagine you've told a friend you need to spend less time with them, but just a couple of days later, they ask to get together.

- Write down three ways you can assertively decline the request.

- Practice saying these in a mirror. Which feels most natural?

SAYING YES

When you assertively communicate to someone that you want to be closer, you help foster growth and make more meaningful connections.

When you reach out to someone, you're making yourself vulnerable—assertive communication involves being explicit about your own wants and needs. Being vulnerable involves three steps: initiating, committing, and following through.

> **BRENÉ BROWN** is a researcher who studies the effects of vulnerability in relationships. She's found that being able to be vulnerable correlates with greater life satisfaction; when people take chances in their relationships, they're likely to be rewarded.

The first step in being vulnerable is putting yourself out there, or initiating. If you don't take a chance, you can't expect the people you're communicating with to do so. In that case, change is less likely, so achieving a relationship that supports your happiness is also less likely.

The second step is committing. It's important that when you decide to take this risk, you don't get cold feet. Staying confident in your communication invites other people to be confident in taking their own risk by opening up to you.

The last step is following through. Vulnerability is not something you do once. You have to choose to do it continually as you open yourself up to new possibilities in your relationships (and to new relationships in general). If you dedicate yourself to this process, you can find happiness in your relationships in new ways.

Vulnerability can be incredibly rewarding, but it takes practice. Nothing new—and that includes happiness—can come into your life if you're unable to open yourself up to it. If you think about occasions when you've gone through a difficult time with friends, family, or partners, you probably resolved the situation by taking a chance. Maybe you decided to forgive them for hurting you or made a major change like giving up an addiction or habit that was affecting your relationship. I'm sure that being vulnerable has paid off sometimes, and sometimes it hasn't. You'll want to practice being vulnerable in your relationships because it is an art form that can be improved. If you open yourself up too much, you might risk getting hurt, but too little and you don't provide enough room for big changes to occur in your relationships. Here is an exercise to help you in doing so.

EXERCISE: PRACTICING VULNERABILITY

- Choose someone you know casually, and think of one quality you appreciate about them.
- Now do the same for someone you know pretty well.
- And the same for someone you are quite close with.

Over the next two to four weeks, find times to share that appreciation with each person.

It's okay to start small when you're learning how to be vulnerable. Every positive experience will help you feel confident enough to take it a step further.

OUT WITH THE OLD, IN WITH THE NEW

As you go about deciding what changes to make in your relationships and developing the skills to do so, one thing that needs to be abundantly clear is that this isn't like ripping a bandage off. When you've been connected to the same people and entrenched in the same relationship patterns for a long time, it's a big adjustment to get used to, for better and for worse. It's important to grieve and get closure on what you've lost. At the same time, you'll want to fully recognize the hope and joy that comes with the changes. Here's an example of what this looks like in practice.

Patricia is both a mother and a grandmother. For the past one and a half years, she has had custody of her three-year-old granddaughter. Her daughter lost custody when her neighbors called the police about loud crying noises, and it was found that she had left her infant daughter unsupervised to pick up more alcohol. Since then, her daughter completed court-mandated treatment and claims she is currently sober.

Patricia made the choice to allow her daughter to visit with her granddaughter once a week after deciding through therapy that it would make her granddaughter happy, which in turn makes her happy. However, she decided not to allow them to leave her supervision, which is something that greatly upset her daughter and her boyfriend.

On the surface, Patricia made the decision that was right for her, and she followed through with it using assertiveness. Now, though, she's dealing with the aftereffects of the changes, and it's getting difficult. When her daughter walks through the door, all the bad memories flood back to her—how lost her daughter was and how painful it was trying to get her back on track for years. She also sees the happiness and laughter of her granddaughter when her mom comes to see her.

Patricia closed the door on trying to be her daughter's savior, when for so long she made it her focus. She opened the door to finding ways to reconnect with her daughter. Patricia took *the time to grieve the relationship and learned to appreciate the new beginning over several months of work.*

Here are some of the things we worked on in the following pages.

OUT WITH THE OLD

When you decide to assertively close or open doors in your relationships, significant change is an inevitable consequence. All your relationships follow certain patterns. By making a new choice, you're changing the pattern, and the relationship must change to adjust (remember systems theory?). Because you're working on becoming happier, this is the perfect time to create new relationship patterns that support your happiness.

When you close a door, you lose whatever that person brought to your life. This can produce mixed feelings. Maybe you didn't want the negativity they brought to your life, but there are bound to be some positives you'll miss, too. In developing happiness, it's important to be able to foster a solid perspective on the choices you make and find peace with them.

To find peace, you need to be aware of the effect any decision has on your life. In what ways has setting a boundary made your life better and healthier? What parts of your life are now emptier? What relationship pattern have you chosen to move on from by letting go of that person?

There are some common negative patterns you might find in your own relationships. The other person might:

- Dominate conversation most of the time
- Be critical or blame you when something goes wrong between you two
- Be jealous of instead of happy for your successes
- Not follow through on commitments

These are just a few examples. The exercises in this chapter so far may have helped you identify others you've been dealing with. By answering these questions and identifying the patterns you're trying to get rid of, you're on the path to resolving lingering feelings and finding closure.

A great way to go about gaining closure is by looking at a relationship in detail. If you can be mindful of the pain you're leaving behind as well as the good things you'll miss and want to replace, the adjustment to life without this relationship will be easier. Think about a time you've had to let go of something that someone said to you that hurt. You didn't all of a sudden not care about what they said; the words still hurt. Somehow you needed to be able to acknowledge how it hurt and move from there. The same thing is true in moving forward from difficult relationships.

You have to acknowledge the hurt while also figuring out how to move on from the hurt, or how it changed you. By doing so, you'll be better able to appreciate the relationship for what it was, both good and bad, without being hindered by trying to bandage an active wound.

Moving forward from the pain allows for good things to grow in its place. Sometimes the greatest heartbreaks are the fertile ground from which brighter futures blossom.

EXERCISE: EMPTYING THE SUITCASE

Imagine coming home from a trip with your suitcase, which represents a relationship you're letting go of.

- List what's in the suitcase (positive, negative, and neutral).
- Which of these items are you going to give away and never think about again?
- Which of these items will you miss?

The mistake people make sometimes is shutting the door and not grieving the loss of the relationship fully. It's important to remember the good parts of this relationship. By recognizing the fullness of it, you'll be able to let go rather than hold on to anger or hurt as you move forward.

IN WITH THE NEW

Not only will you want to reflect on the gravity of closing a door, but you'll also want to embrace the opportunities the newly empty space in your life provides. Envisioning exciting possibilities is a good way to build the confidence you need to fill your life with happiness.

For every negative dynamic you lose, you can find something positive to replace it with. What's positive for you will depend on what your core values are and who you want to be.

Let's talk about a few healthy relationship patterns you may want to seek out as you form new connections.

- Listen attentively to each other.
- Encourage each other in new pursuits.
- Offer candid but caring critique when asked for feedback or when concerned about a certain behavior.
- Be reliable.

Think about the people you named in the *Keeping Doors Open* exercise. Take a minute to reflect on how they fit into these patterns or others you can identify.

Now that you know what types of relationships you'd like to pursue, you have to be brave enough to start chasing them. Sometimes the biggest mistake we make is waiting for good things to come to us. We need to find them for ourselves.

Opening new doors is necessary for growth, but it's always a risk. It's important to be aware of your worries so that they don't hold you back. The best way to do this is with mindfulness.

Remember the cognitive distortion of magnifying/minimizing from rule #1? Often our tendency is to see the negatives and ignore the positives. This is more likely when you're afraid or worried. This skill will help you move through uncertainty as you change the relationships you have and build new ones.

EXERCISE: MINDFUL REFRAMING

Get two jars of similar size and several small slips of paper.

- Write down fears, worries, and negative beliefs you have about the new relationships you want to invite into your life. Put them in one jar.
- Now write down positive thoughts, feelings, and beliefs about those relationships. Put them in the other jar. Continue writing positive things until the positives jar is noticeably more full.

While this might seem simple, it helps teach you something complex: cognitive reframing. Cognitive reframing is taking a negative thought or feeling and transforming it into something more positive.

CONTINUING IN CONNECTION

Having learned the skills you need to retune your relationships, it's time to explore how to maintain your progress. The following skills are meant to help you make lasting changes, not just short-term ones, in your connections with others.

You know how to process the changes you've made and emotionally adjust to them. The last step in finding your people is staying connected to them, or more specifically, connecting to them in such a way that your relationships continue to be healthy and full of happiness. To do this, you'll need to continually monitor your communication, maintain gratitude, and establish shared meaning. Here's an example of what this looks like in practice.

Mark and Cheryl, recent newlyweds, were both previously married. They sought therapy to make sure "they weren't making the same mistakes." Mark starts to analyze himself, all his tendencies and faults in relationships with others, and Cheryl does the same. They've both clearly been in therapy before. Everything that we discussed so far in rules #1 and #2, they've worked on extensively.

In the midst of their analysis of themselves, one thing is abundant. They're so concerned with how they'll "bring the relationship down" that they haven't thought about how they're going to build it up in the first place, and then maintain that growth.

What Mark and Cheryl needed to do wasn't necessarily to change something in the relationship but rather to add to it. They developed a way of communicating with each other specifically focused on talking about their relationship, decided the meaning they wanted their relationship to be built on, and practiced having a constant attitude of gratefulness for one another.

Over time, as they continued to put effort into this process, they noticed that their relationship anxiety and their fears associated with divorce began to subside.

The main thing these exercises all share is that they serve as a reminder that no one person should or has to carry the burden of making the relationship work. When you work with all the people in your life to maintain relationship health, nothing will slow you down. Here are exercises to get you started.

BUILDING RELATIONSHIPS

Being your best in your relationships requires active participation if you're looking to find happiness in them.

So what does it mean to actively participate in your relationships? It means that you dedicate time and attention to the people you're close to. You can't get far on your own. If you want people to accompany you as you create a happier life, you have to do the same for them.

There are many ways to show someone you care, but one of the most effective is to be as invested in their growth as you are in your own. What are they working toward? What will make them happy? Discovering your core values helped you unlock the understanding you needed to make changes in your own life. By exploring another's values and goals, you'll be able to support them.

The best way to discover what a friend cares about is to simply ask them. Asking good questions is an art form. Your goal is to invite them to share as much about themselves as they're comfortable with. For questions to be effective, they need to be open-ended, tactful, and compassionate.

Open-ended questions encourage multiple answers, whereas closed questions have limited options for answering. An example of a closed question that is ineffective is "Have things been going well lately?" This question has two possible answers: yes or no. If you instead ask, "How have things been going for you lately?" you're allowing the person to give more detail and share their experience, which will teach you much more about them.

To be tactful, consider how your timing, delivery, and choice of phrasing affects the response. If you ask someone about themselves before a test, you might receive a tense response. However, if you ask during their downtime, they're likely more open to sharing.

Do you remember a time as a kid when you asked for something from your parents or guardian? I imagine you tried to catch them in a good mood and tried to get on their good side. Doing the same thing as you get older isn't so much different. Understanding the person you're talking to and how they're feeling is key in knowing how to approach them. Ask questions about how they're feeling in the moment to be able to gauge them. Questions like "How have you been feeling today?" or "What did life bring you today, and how are you dealing with it?" can be great ways to allow people to invite you into their current frame of mind.

A team of Finnish researchers led by **AINO SAARINEN,** in one of the first major studies on the topic of compassion, tracked thousands of individuals over 15 years and found that higher levels of compassion predicted higher levels of long-term well-being.

The most important aspect of getting to know someone is compassion. You will never fully understand what another person is going through, but in seeking to understand by asking thoughtful questions, you can demonstrate compassion in every interaction. To do this, consider how your words will be received by the other person. Does the question you're asking show genuine interest? Does it convey that who they are and what they're going through matters? Ask yourself these questions before you start asking questions to another person.

EXERCISE: ASKING GOOD QUESTIONS

Think of a recent interaction you had with someone.

- Write down two questions that either of you asked during the conversation.
- Evaluate these questions. How do or don't they fit the standards explained in this section?
- Rewrite the questions so they are open-ended, tactful, and compassionate.

Great connections are founded in great questions. Sometimes asking about someone's life in an effective way can have a great impact. You've likely experienced it yourself. Think about a time where you were having a really bad day, and someone asked you how you were feeling. There likely have been times when it didn't help, but when it did, it was probably because they asked you while expressing considerable care and compassion. This is a great reason to practice asking questions meaningfully.

CREATING GRATITUDE

As you work on developing stronger relationships, it's important to also develop gratitude. It's easy to start taking the people in your life for granted, but it's better to learn how to appreciate the ways they support your own happiness. Practicing gratitude for your friends, partners, and even coworkers or fellow students boosts your own well-being and improves your relationships.

> **GLENN FOX,** who researches the neuroscience of gratitude, has found that the practice correlates to greater social bonding and stress relief.

What do the relationships you choose to foster mean to you? What qualities of the people in your life do you most appreciate? Having a clear motivation fuels every behavior. Being grateful for your relationships motivates you to invest in them.

Practicing gratitude is challenging because the world has a way of making the flaws or shortcomings in our relationships seem more pressing. And while it's important to work on what's going wrong, it's equally important to appreciate what's going right. When people are going through tough times, often all we hear from friends are condolences. How often do people recognize your resilience in all of it? The world tends to focus on how we're hurting, but let's make sure you're grateful for the strong person you are while you're working things out.

A good way to practice gratitude is to find a method of recording what you're grateful for. Tracking these thoughts will help remind you what you're fighting when you're struggling in a relationship.

There are a lot of gratitude apps out there, but they don't all help you focus on the specifics of your life. Options that do prompt you to notice what you appreciate about your people are 365 Gratitude, Grateful, Presently, Bliss, and Longwalks. Some of these allow you to share your entries with friends and family, while others provide more education about the value of gratitude.

Or if you want to do it the classic way, get a notebook and start a gratitude journal!

EXERCISE: GRATITUDE JOURNAL

Use these prompts to get you started with your own gratitude journal. As you build your gratitude practice, you'll find other experiences you want to record.

- Who made my day better? How?
- Did someone surprise me today?
- When did I feel someone listened to me?
- What do I admire most about (choose a friend, partner, or family member)?
- Did I receive a compliment today?
- Which friend supports my goals and how?
- Which professor helps me learn?
- What have I learned about communication from (choose a friend, partner, or family member)?
- Who is showing me what love looks like? How?

There are countless lists of gratitude prompts online, but these will get you started on the path of expressing gratitude specifically for the people in your life.

SHARING PURPOSE

All your relationships need to hold clear direction and purpose. Just like you have explored the direction you want to take, you need to be aware of where your relationships are headed. To take meaningful steps in a relationship, your relationship needs to have . . . meaning. What are you and the people in your life working toward in life as a team, and why?

The relationships you have need to be solid, and for you to have a solid relationship with another person, you need to have direction. If a relationship doesn't have movement toward a greater purpose, it's stagnant. Being stagnant is not an option when it comes to happiness because life is not a stagnant process. Life will keep moving whether you like it or not, and if your relationships don't move with the natural challenges you'll face, such as aging, you'll be stuck, unable to keep making progress.

This is not a one-and-done process. Your relationship's meanings will shift as you continue to grow. It's important to regularly take inventory of how things are going. That will help you decide how and when you need to reevaluate the "mission statement" of each relationship in your life.

The best times to take a close look at your relationships are when you are at your highest and lowest points in your search for happiness. These intense moments hold opportunity for you to learn what relationship dynamics affect you the most. When a relationship is suffering, your assessment of its value will teach you what makes your relationships work—or not. When a relationship is feeling easy and strong, you'll also learn what's important to foster and what you might need to let go of.

So when you're closing and opening doors, using assertiveness, inviting healthy relationship patterns into your life, and building new connections, keep in mind that your relationships, like you, will evolve. This chapter provides the tools for you to create mutually supportive relationships that will grow your happiness even during life's uncertainties.

EXERCISE: MUTUAL MEANING

Think about the important relationships in your life.

1. Why are you connected to this person?

2. Why do you continue to stay connected?

3. What can you do to ensure the purpose that this relationship has continues to be served?

This is a simple way to be able to evaluate how each relationship plays into the grand scheme of your life. This leads us into the next rule of chaotic happiness that will be discussed in the next chapter: finding your purpose.

CHAPTER LEARNINGS

- Identifying who in your life weighs you down and who supports you is an important step for happiness.
- As you consider your relationships, think about the effort each person puts in. Are you both investing energy?
- Ending relationships requires you to expect, engage, and execute the change.
- Learning to communicate assertively will help you in both holding boundaries and building connection.
- Fostering the relationships you have means being vulnerable, but the payoff is worth it.
- Be aware of what relationship patterns you are letting go of and which ones you want to hold onto.
- Use what you've learned about your existing relationships to figure out how to create new relationships.
- To build healthy connections, focus on asking questions that are open-ended, tactful, and compassionate.
- Practicing gratitude will strengthen your relationships as well as your own well-being.
- Check in regularly with yourself about the shared purpose in your relationships and how they are affecting you.

RULE #3: FIND YOUR PURPOSE

When you're looking for happiness in a world with uncertainty, it's crucial to know what your purpose is. Purpose is like a magnifying glass that helps you focus your life. When there's so much going on around you in the world, purpose helps you keep your eye on the prize: happiness. When you decide on a purpose, you won't get thrown off course by a world where nothing is set in stone.

WHAT THE WORLD WANTS FROM YOU

You might be starting this chapter with a sense of your place in the world. But is that sense your own, or did someone (like your parents or a teacher) give it to you? The world places expectations on all of us. We're all under pressure to meet those expectations, to fit in and not stand out. But it's important that you understand how the world's expectations of you do or don't line up with what you want for yourself in the world. How do you want to participate in the world to build your own happy life?

Even when you find yourself and find the right people in life, there will be times when you have to deal with the outside world and you don't have control over what happens. The last rule of chaotic happiness is about finding your purpose. You need to have a solid understanding of how you're going to make an impact in the world at large, in addition to your own world.

To do this, you'll first want to think about what society expects of you. How much are you willing and able to conform to that, and what do you want to fight against?

Let's start with an example.

> Bryce is a student who's not been doing well in class recently. His teachers advised his parents to seek counseling after an incident in which he got frustrated with his math teacher, flipped off his teacher, and stormed out of the room. Bryce's parents were mortified and stunned that this happened. He's never like this at home, and they would've never imagined that he'd do something like this.
>
> His parents keep insisting he's a good person and apologize on his behalf, but his teachers think he might need to transfer to a behavioral program. Bryce, on the other hand, doesn't talk to anyone. As soon as he gets to school, he puts his head down on the desk, and when he comes home, he goes straight to his own room.
>
> During his first counseling session, Bryce asks me how he can be "fixed" and be "less of a problem" because that's the language he's hearing at home and at school. I tell him what I tell most kids in his position: "I don't think there's really anything about you that needs fixing."
>
> Bryce clearly has ADHD; that's why he's getting so frustrated, especially when it comes to detail-oriented subjects such as math. However, verbal aggression cannot be his answer to

how he deals with it. Society expects him to be cooperative and nonaggressive, and that will never change. At the same time, we can acknowledge that his teachers can work with him to accommodate his ADHD by allowing him to take breaks, etc. There is room for change in that.

Bryce started to become less frustrated, and more important he also felt heard. He could both fit into others' expectations of him and find ways for exceptions to be made so that he could find his balance.

Here are some exercises to guide you on the path to doing the same.

FITTING IN

Why do we so deeply crave fitting in? Because we need to feel like we belong. The desire to conform is a human instinct based on the need to survive. The security of knowing you're a part of something bigger than yourself has immense value.

How does fitting in play a role in finding happiness? When we're looking for happiness in social structures such as school, the workplace, our friend group, or the larger community, we're hoping for approval. We think acceptance will make us happy, but fitting in doesn't necessarily mean you're being true to your own values, wants, and needs.

Fitting in means you're compatible with other members of a group in a certain context. There's no one way to fit in—it varies from situation to situation. The important thing is to make sure that fitting in supports the person you're working to become. For instance, if your friend group frequently talks negatively of other people or if you find that your workplace doesn't operate with similar values to your own, fitting in could seriously jeopardize your happiness. Conformity may be a natural human instinct, but please don't try to fit in at your own expense. Be aware that you don't mirror the world's toxicity. If we go along with the crowd all the time, we're in serious trouble.

For example, maybe your core values are advocating for environmentalism and social justice. For you to shape a world with more equity, you'll need to break with the majority to fight for it. It's natural for many people not to be conscious of their carbon footprint, but if you ignore it, too, you're keenly aware there won't be a world for anyone to exist in at all. This all goes to show that it's just as important to do things differently than to fit in.

You can develop your understanding of when you might want to fit in and when you might not by practicing self-observation. Self-observation is about adopting more distanced awareness of what you're thinking and doing. By observing yourself in the world, you can better recognize how your desire to fit in is affecting you. Here is an exercise to help you develop this technique.

EXERCISE: SELF-OBSERVATION

When you're in a public place or social situation, ask yourself:

1. How does your behavior change? Do you find yourself talking, thinking, or feeling differently than you usually do?
2. If you do notice differences, which differences stick out to you the most, and why?
3. Do these differences have an overall positive or negative effect on you as a person?

For this exercise to be effective, it's important that you repeat it several times in different situations. The first time you might not get a lot out of it, but that's okay. This set of questions, when asked repeatedly, will help you learn to notice your "fitting in" behavior. Once you understand your patterns, you can make judgment calls about when to fit in and when doing so doesn't support your happiness.

STANDING OUT

When fitting in is detrimental to the person you want to be, the alternative is to stand out. After all, you can't expect to find true happiness by being a pretend version of yourself. Choosing to stand out is a positive social contribution. When we all offer different strengths and skills, our communities have what they need to thrive, and the world is a healthier and more diverse place.

While we might be more true to ourselves when we stand out, it's not something we always know how to do. Breaking away from the pack might help us become happier people, but it also can create conflict.

For example, let's say you're the introvert in your friend group. You need alone time to recharge and focus on an activity you love. Your friends might be disappointed when you turn down their invitations, but you're staying true to your own needs. I hope you have the kind of friends who will understand and keep inviting you anyway.

Consider what you have to gain from going out on your own rather than following what everyone else is doing. You give yourself the opportunity to make an impact on others in new and unique ways. You're the only you who has ever existed, so you might as well start acting like it. The innovation and changes we need to create a better world, like mentioned before, won't come from being just like everyone else all the time. You also might find that by taking a stand of your own, you gain a sense of ownership in the things you do. Suddenly life becomes a lot more meaningful and interesting when you're being yourself for reasons completely your own.

Being different always carries some risk. People criticize what they can't understand, but that's not a reason to be any less extraordinary in your particular way. Being extraordinary is part of being happy.

You may be wondering how the ways in which you stand out affect you and those around you. The next exercise will help you explore the impact of your differences.

EXERCISE: INTERNAL AND EXTERNAL IMPACT

Get a sheet of paper and make two columns: one for internal impact and one for external impact.

1. **Internal Impact**

   A. **Think about one way in which you stand out.**

   B. **How does being different in this way affect the ways you think and feel about yourself?**

   C. **What would be the consequences for you if you were to change this part of yourself to be more like other people? Positive or negative?**

2. **External Impact**

   A. **Think about the same quality.**

   B. **How does being different in this way affect how other people see or experience you?**

   C. **What would be the consequences for the world if you were to change this part of yourself to be more like other people? Positive or negative?**

Consider the net impact, internal and external, of the quality you chose to analyze. The point of this exercise is to start seeing the value in the ways you stand out. Your differences often require the most courage to embrace and develop.

UNDERSTANDING EXPECTATIONS

Sometimes, without even knowing it, we end up living the life other people want for us rather than finding and living the one we want for ourselves. You might wonder, *Am I just like everyone else, or am I different?* This is a common question. It's not like anyone explains in school what it means to fit in or stand out. What we have instead are implicit rules. These unspoken expectations cause anxiety and uncertainty.

For example, let's say you go to a party. There is basic party etiquette (be polite, make conversation, etc.), but each person in the room will have slightly different unspoken expectations. One person might think it's appropriate to talk about light things like favorite TV shows, while another will want to get into deeper discussions about climate change. Whether or not you meet someone's expectations will depend on what you want to talk about, and there's no way to know. A lot of you might worry about these social interactions ahead of time, and you're likely to feel uncomfortable in the moment if you sense someone is unsatisfied with your interaction.

Anticipating when we will fit in or stand out is difficult when people's expectations vary. So how do you account for this? How do you fill in the blanks so that you can be the best version of yourself in the real world? The answer is simple: you don't. You don't figure out every nuance of what other people expect. Instead, you choose how to engage based on your own values and expectations of yourself.

At the party, for instance, you might be one of the people who wants deeper interaction but finds yourself chatting with someone who wants to talk about their favorite TV shows. In that context, you're standing out by taking the conversation to a serious place, but that's okay because you're staying true to what you care about. You might be at the party to build connections with people in the community who are involved in local activism. Once you find one of those people to talk to, you'll be fitting in.

Your focus should be on the expectations that align most closely with your own core values. Let's do an exercise comparing values and expectations.

EXERCISE: VALUES AND EXPECTATIONS

Think back to the core values you discovered in rule #1. Recall some of the expectations other people (your parents, your friends, or your partner) have of you.

1. In what ways are these expectations in line with how you want to engage with the world?

2. In what ways do these expectations conflict with who you want to be in your community?

The purpose of this exercise is to help you identify how external expectations do or don't line up with your core self. It's important that the expectations you choose to meet align with your values. You won't become happy by living up to other people's standards.

WHAT YOU WANT FROM THE WORLD

Not only do you get to decide how to fit into the world, but you also get to choose what you want to put into your experience of being alive. There are many ways in which you need to follow the same paths to be a part of society, but the best part is paving new ones for yourself. By creating new paths, you are able to express yourself to the fullest extent. In order to do so, it's important to decide what you want first.

Mariah has spent the last few years working to graduate from high school and college as quickly as possible. She did it, and now she's completely unsure of what she wants to do with the rest of her life. For so long she had her sights set on being the best student. At this point, she's not sure if she should continue by going to grad school, or if it's time to take another path.

She's decided to come to therapy because she feels stuck and wants some guidance regarding what she should do next. Fortunately and unfortunately for Mariah, that isn't how this works. The best person to decide what Mariah should do . . . is Mariah. What I can do is give her a framework to assist her in her process of discovering the choice she wants to make.

I encourage Mariah to consider the work we did regarding core beliefs, as well as the health of her relationships. What is it that she cares about? How does she like to help others? What gives her life meaning? She answers these questions by saying that she cares about being connected and making sure her people are healthy and happy—that's what matters most to her. The question then becomes how she can offer that to the rest of the world.

Eventually, it became clear she wants to continue her education and go to medical school. She created an action plan for how she wanted to accomplish that and developed strategies for herself to stay motivated through the process.

This careful consideration is exactly what I'm going to ask you to do, too.

FINDING PURPOSE

Knowing what you want from the world is even more important than knowing what the world wants from you. Finding happiness means pursuing your goals even when the world doesn't support you. Taking uncertain steps into the unknown is risky and scary. You'll need to be intentional about making choices that help you stay focused and find ways to motivate yourself when you lose sight of the path.

You've already done some work to understand who you want to be and what's important to you in relationships. But what will fulfill you? What will give your life meaning? What do you need to achieve to be happy? These are big questions, but it boils down to purpose. At its deepest level, purpose is what gives life meaning. If that's too existential for you, think of purpose as a long-term goal that is both significant to you and makes a positive contribution to the world. Purpose is knowing what you need to do to be fulfilled by your life. Happiness lies in being your best self for your own joy, your relationships, *and* the world.

VIKTOR FRANKL developed logotherapy. This is the idea that the search for meaning drives all humans. Finding meaning and purpose strengthens resilience and promotes well-being.

We explored congruence in rule #1, and that applies here. Living purposefully requires living in accordance with your core values. Because these values are the foundation of what you find meaningful, they will help you face adversity in an indifferent world.

The mistake most people make when considering what they want is not digging deep enough. They only think about the tangible things and don't explore what they care most about, or they know what that is, but don't spend time figuring out how to prioritize it.

For example, you may have been advised to choose a future-proof job that you don't necessarily derive a lot of personal value from—you learned a skill set that is supposed to be relevant for at least the next 10 years. Doing so might help your job stability, but will it fulfill you? What if the world is so different in 10 years that the skill set you developed to maintain a career isn't useful anymore? All that effort you put into a surface goal—having a career—has not set you up to continue living a meaningful life in a totally different context.

Your purpose can also be entirely separate from the work you do to pay the bills. Some people find purpose in raising children, pursuing a creative practice, or committing to activism. If your purpose is founded in your core values, you're more likely to experience long-term happiness. The next exercise will help you explore that connection.

EXERCISE: VALUES-BASED PURPOSE

Imagine it's five years in the future and you are living a happy life.

1. What's most satisfying about your daily life?
2. What do you put most of your time and energy into?
3. What's different between your present life and your future life?
4. What would the people in your future life say about you?
5. What would your future self say about you?
6. Can you identify one to three things that have become the central theme of your life in five years?

If you're struggling with these questions, that's okay. I recommend thinking about them over the course of a few days or weeks. Sometimes we get so stuck on where we are now that we struggle to see how things could be different. Imagining a future version of yourself creates the psychological distance necessary to start picturing what life is like outside that stuckness.

When you are using your time and energy to actualize your values, you will have a foundation for happiness no matter how unpredictable the world is.

ACTING WITH INTENTION

Once you know your purpose, you have to pursue it. You'll need to be intentional in making choices that move you closer to living that purpose. Intent means you stick to your goals without wavering. It doesn't mean that you never switch your style or strategy, but rather that you keep your eyes on the prize.

Just by focusing on the purpose you set for yourself, you're more likely to fulfill it every day. Have you ever heard the term *manifesting*? Intentionality is the key ingredient that makes manifesting—the practice of visualizing what you want to make a reality—work. When you keep it in your mind's eye to live a certain way or for certain reasons, actions tend to follow. If you don't pursue your purpose with intentionality, it's a lot less likely to manifest in how you live your life. If purpose is a door to more happiness in the world, then intentionality is the key that opens it.

Intentionality requires single-mindedness. Everything you do must serve to bring you closer to fulfilling your purpose. This means no wasting energy, shifting your attention to a new hobby, or getting sidetracked by what your best friend or parents think you should do. This may seem intense, but think of it this way: if you want maximum happiness, you'll need to give maximum effort to chasing it.

To be single-minded, you'll likely need to make some adjustments to your daily life. This isn't something you'll do once, but rather a thousand times. The world has a way of distracting you, but learning to be single-minded in your efforts is the only way to fulfill your purpose, which is a necessary foundation for happiness. Think about it . . . if you can't be committed 100 percent to your purpose, how are you supposed to be successful?

Take for example someone whose purpose is to be the world's greatest basketball player. If they're only committed to their purpose 90 percent of the time, what's going to happen when things get difficult and they encounter trials? Without that 10 percent commitment, they're more likely going to quit when their purpose is challenged on the tough days. Being single-minded is one of the best ways to live with intention, and it's a skill that requires practice. Here's an exercise to get started.

EXERCISE: SINGLE-MINDEDNESS

1. Make a list of all the things you do in an average week.

2. Cross off what you have to do for survival (like eating and sleeping).

3. Cross off what you do for others that doesn't bring you happiness.

4. Cross off what you do for yourself that doesn't bring you happiness.

5. Cross off what you do that's boring.

6. Circle what's left.

How much of what you do is about your purpose? Look at what your crossed off in questions three through five. What if you devoted all the energy you currently put into those things instead toward pursuing your purpose with single-mindedness? Take a look at what your circled in question six. If there's not much you do throughout the day that brings you happiness, that's an indicator you need to be more single-minded. You might think that focusing all your energy on the purpose that brings you happiness is selfish, but it's quite the opposite. When you focus on the things you circled last, you're going to be better and more fully equipped to benefit others around you than you would otherwise.

The takeaway here is that you need to be aware and conscious of the importance of what you're focusing on. Ultimately this will be key in determining the amount of happiness you have.

STAYING MOTIVATED

Being intentional with your focus on purpose will help you be able to fulfill it. However, you'll also need to maintain motivation. Without it, a single-minded focus on your purpose won't get you anywhere. Think about any athletic competition. Most of the athletes spend similar amounts of time practicing and competing, but only a few win. Additionally, in the workplace, employees might spend about the same amount of time at the office, but not everyone excels at their job.

A key difference between those who fulfill their purpose and those who don't is motivation. Motivation is the energy that gives you the ability to be productive and make progress. The more motivated you are, the more likely it is you'll make significant progress in fulfilling your purpose day by day. It's also an important part of withstanding unpredictable circumstances. You never know what's going to happen in the uncertain world, and sometimes you're going to need a lot of energy to power through hard times.

To be more motivated or to find motivation in the first place, you need to be creative. The things that motivate you won't remain the same every day because the challenges you face change frequently. Of the things you're working on right now, some of them may have challenged you for awhile, and some of them might be brand new. Different challenges require different approaches, but the motivation to meet these challenges can always come from your purpose. For example, someone might struggle with anxiety more one day and depression more the next. The approach a person takes to tackle each of these will be different. However, the motivation that gives them the strength to work on each comes from their purpose.

The reason for this has to do with how you prioritize things in your life. You can't focus on a bunch of different things at the same time. However, you can focus on the most important thing, your purpose, and stay motivated by connecting the challenges you face to that purpose. Like when someone needs to mow the lawn, they might find the motivation to do so by remembering that providing an orderly home to live in helps fulfill their purpose of building a strong family. So, let's practice making these connections for yourself. The next exercise will help you find motivation.

EXERCISE: FINDING MOTIVATION

Take some time to think about something you have to do that you've struggled to be motivated for recently.

1. What do you think the qualities are of this task that make it more difficult to get motivated to do it?

2. Was it always like this? Has there ever been a time when it wasn't so difficult?

3. How might you connect this thing to your deeper purpose?

Write down the connections you've made and refer to them whenever you have to do the thing you're currently struggling with. By consistently making the things you struggle with meaningful and connected to your purpose, you'll start to notice you have more energy to do them.

If you're having trouble connecting your struggles to your purpose, try seeing this exercise like a jigsaw puzzle. The more pieces there are, the more difficult it is to configure the picture. For a long time, finding your motivation might look like a pile of puzzle pieces that don't fit together. The key is in understanding that everything you do, you do for a reason. If you can master your actions by making them all meaningful and connected to your purpose, you'll have an unlimited supply of energy.

LAYING THE GROUNDWORK

Knowing how to cope with the world's expectations while having an idea of what you're hoping to gain is an important step. An equally important step is preparing yourself for the work it takes to follow through with these things. Getting yourself in the right place mentally is the next important step you'll need to take so you can find your purpose.

Eli hates his job with a passion. The hours are long, the pay is low, and he feels unappreciated all the time. He's coming to therapy because he's been experiencing a lot of anxiety around this recently. He wants to leave, but he doesn't feel like he can. If he leaves this job, what if he can't get the job that he wants?

So he's at a crossroad between the place he knows he doesn't want to be and the place he's unsure he can get to. The most important thing for him to work on right now is laying the groundwork and plotting out his course, even though he's bound to trip and fall at least a little.

Most important, what we work on in therapy is finding the right structure. What's going to continually motivate Eli to pursue the things he identifies as being important to his happiness? This is important because in the pursuit of these things, it's likely that conflicts will come along that could knock him off his path, such as a job market drought or not having the right contacts.

The main focus here is on the skill of stabilizing himself should one of these roadblocks find him, as well as just embracing the process entirely.

While the challenges you meet in the outside world may be different from Eli's challenges, you'll need the same skills. Let's take a deeper look.

STABILIZING

Once you know what your purpose is and how to actualize it, you have to set yourself up for success. You can't make big changes without a stable baseline that will hold you up when life gets hard. As you start committing to your purpose, make sure you know what gives you that stability and how to pay close attention to the possibilities in front of you.

The first step is to find your footing before you take action. It may seem ironic that the first step you take toward fulfilling your purpose is standing still, but I assure you it's not. Establishing a foothold of stability—a place of peace—will help you get through the uncertainty to come.

So what does this foothold or place look like? It's different for different people. The idea is to have a thought or an activity—a TV show, exercise, art, or craft—or even a physical location that serves as a haven.

The purpose of having a place of peace as you leave your comfort zone is replenishment. The world is going to challenge you. You might even find yourself back at the starting point. When this happens, you need to have a place where you can heal and prepare to get back into the game quickly. People sometimes give up on succeeding because they feel so defeated they can't find a way to bounce back—and they haven't prepared for this by knowing what they need to recover.

This place offers your mind a chance to rest and temporarily forget your worries. It feels safe. A foothold of stability that some people hold close is watching streamed TV and movies. In moderation, watching Netflix or Hulu can decrease overthinking and encourage stillness. For others, spending quality time with a close friend, reading a favorite book, doodling, or taking a short trip into the woods will give them the respite they need.

Knowing how to use your foothold will be your secret weapon in facing the difficult road. When something unexpected happens or you fail at something important, it's time to go to your place of peace. Next is an exercise to help you understand this tool.

EXERCISE: PLACES OF PEACE

1. What are your footholds of stability or places of peace?

2. Why do these give you comfort and reenergize you?

3. When you're stressed, at what point do you need to visit these places?

4. What can you do to incorporate more rest into your life?

These questions will help you strategize. We all have places of peace, but we don't always remember to use them to our advantage. Taking time to rest and recover helps you stay focused on what you care most about.

DEVELOPING INSIGHT

As you focus more on working toward your goals, you'll need to sharpen your insight, or your ability to sense connections and understand things at a deeper level. The most successful people have a way of predicting what might happen next. They have the gift of knowing when to seize an opportunity. They're able to do this because they understand associations—potential and possible outcomes of a big choice and connections between thoughts and emotions, for instance.

Cultivating insight will help you learn from your mistakes, understand challenges as you face them, and better sense what choices will help keep your focus where it needs to be. Insight is a tool that requires drawing on past experiences to inform your decisions in the present. Have you ever met someone who repeatedly makes the same mistake? Someone who keeps forgiving the same people who turn around and hurt them again? Or a person who continually makes the same error at work? Using insight will help you avoid costly mistakes like these.

Insight is particularly important to finding happiness because it not only helps you determine what *not* to do, but it also tells you the things you *should* do. If something has worked out for you in the past or benefited you, you'll likely have a similar outcome if you repeat the same steps that led to your success. Think about when you're trying to learn to play an instrument or improve your study habits. As you continue to work at these things, you slowly notice tips and tricks for yourself that make you better. If this is true on a smaller scale, wouldn't it make sense that this same principle applies to something as large as finding the best way to live out your purpose?

To develop the insight, you'll need to spend a lot of time reflecting. The more time you spend reflecting on your past and present choices and behaviors, the more you'll notice things that will help guide you. You'll notice patterns, like when you drink coffee while studying, you're more productive. You'll also develop better attention to detail, and doing so will help you notice things you maybe didn't right away that could lead to major breakthroughs. Like if you struggled to stay in tune while singing and then noticed that a certain anxiety made your neck too tense. Using insight helps you get the most from working toward your purpose by ensuring you're always making progress.

The choices you make will always have unpredictable outcomes, but whatever happens, insight guarantees that you'll always be learning. To always keep moving forward in pursuing your purpose is critical to happiness, and continuing to learn helps you do that. The following exercise will help you practice the necessary reflection to improve your insight.

EXERCISE: INSIGHT PRACTICE

1. **Past Reflection**

   A. Visualize the work you've done so far to find happiness.

   B. Be aware of the thoughts and feelings you experienced in those situations.

   C. Now think about these things for five minutes and write down what you learn.

2. **Present Reflection**

   A. Visualize all the work you're currently doing to find happiness.

   B. Be aware of the thoughts and feelings you're experiencing.

   C. Now think about these things for five minutes and write down what you learn.

3. **Future Reflection**

   A. Visualize the work you'll need to do to find happiness.

   B. Be aware of the thoughts and feelings you might experience.

   C. Now think about these things for five minutes and write down what you learn.

The key with this exercise is attention. By learning how to better direct your attention, you're more likely to pick up on things you might otherwise miss. Maybe you pieced together what's been working and what's not. Maybe you haven't started to notice anything at all yet. It might help you to think about the same thing happening in growing relationships. At first you don't notice someone's good or bad patterns, but then you think about it and find things to work on together. Whether you've noticed a lot about what's bringing you happiness or not a lot at all, if you keep working at it, you'll start to pick up things that will serve you on your journey.

To develop good insight, you might want to make this a weekly practice. You'll know you're learning this skill when you can observe how your emotions influence your actions without letting your emotions decide for you. Insight helps you make choices that will support your happiness.

EMBRACING THE PROCESS

It's important to find joy in working toward your purpose. To enjoy doing something simply for the sake of doing it without being too attached to outcomes is the mark of a happy person. The less reliant you are on external rewards, the more likely you'll find lasting happiness. The more conditions you place on what being happy requires, the harder it will be to reach—and stay in—that state. Understand that feeling happy and being happy are not the same thing. Feeling happy is a mood, and all moods change. Chaotic happiness is about learning how to be happy in every circumstance, especially when it's difficult. Feeling happy is great. I hope you feel happy many times over. However, maintaining a feeling of happiness requires work. To do this work, you'll need to enjoy the process itself. Otherwise, you're likely to burn out.

To enjoy the process is to relish the feeling of being alive so that joy is always available. It can be deeply rewarding to chase what matters to you wholeheartedly. Living this way is likely to bring about more satisfaction and happy moments even before you feel like you've "made it." Even little moments of happiness can give you an invaluable boost to prevent you from getting overwhelmed by a persistently uncertain world.

Motivational Interviewing is a therapeutic modality focused on connecting to the process of change. Its creators, **WILLIAM MILLER** and **STEPHEN ROLLNICK,** explain the premise simply: The more we can talk about change, the more it tends to happen.

The joy to be found in the process is more than just a lifeline. It's an existential declaration. Every time you put energy into improving yourself, you're celebrating your commitment to happiness. Life doesn't come with a map. Exploring all it has to offer, even when it feels like you're stumbling in the dark, is empowering. The next exercise will help you reflect on your journey toward a purposeful life and where you have found happiness so far.

EXERCISE: ENJOYING THE PROCESS

Think back to things or experiences you identified in the Insight Practice exercise Past Reflection. Choose one or two.

1. What went well and felt good about those?
2. When something became difficult, how did you convince yourself it was still worth it?
3. How did you continue working toward your goals, even when you felt defeated?
4. What did you appreciate about the process itself?
5. How can you use this awareness to improve the satisfaction you get from your happiness work?

These reflection questions are meant to remind you that even in difficulty, there is much joy to be found. Trying your best and enjoying the small steps that lead to big change are fundamental to a happy life.

WALK AND THEN RUN

To follow through with what you're chasing in the outside world takes a lot of skill. Another thing that will be important as you continue on your journey is learning to maintain your progress. People are often hyperfocused on getting to the "end" of their journey to finding happiness. This is a mistake that hinders your progress. I'm sure you've heard it before, but happiness is not about the destination . . . happiness is about the journey.

Clichés aside, in order to enjoy the journey, it's necessary to take it all in and, with what you take in, to make adjustments to stay on the path of happiness. A better way to illustrate this would be to think of a mountain climber who checks the footholds as they're climbing. It's important to routinely monitor what you're doing and incorporate your actions into your skill set so you don't slip and fall.

> A good example is Nora. She's definitely one of my oldest clients, but she doesn't act like it. She goes to classes at the gym, salsa dances with her also 80-year-old husband, and has more grandkids than I do pairs of socks. She always has a smile. Regardless, I ask the same question that I ask all of my clients: "What are you wanting to talk about today?"
>
> She says, "I actually don't have a lot to talk about today." You see, I've been working with Nora for over a year now. She spent many years not working through abuse she experienced at an early age. Now, though, after a lot of processing, she feels like she's been given a second chance at life and a major load is off her back. You might be wondering why she continues to come to therapy.
>
> What Nora knows and what I know, too, is that progress isn't permanent, and nor is it meant to be. To be truly happy is about continuing to meet the challenges of the world and coming up with new solutions for each one.

That's what it takes to be happy, and that's why this is the last step in the process of chaotic happiness. It's not the end of the journey, but the passing of the torch to you in your continued efforts. Let's take one last look at some things to be mindful of here.

LEARNING TO WALK

Knowing how to pace yourself is essential. Building slowly and steadily will help you learn how to apply your insight and develop more trust in yourself. The changes you make can't solidify if you're moving too fast to think them through. When you find your happiness, you'll want to stay there.

Sometimes the forward steps you take will be challenging, even if they're positive. By exercising patience, you'll be able to consider what you've learned in this chapter so far and apply your new insight to the choices you make.

When pacing yourself, consider how big the change you want to make is. If it's a simple thing like a new hairstyle, the consequences are minor, even if you shave your head. There's no need to put too much thought into that. But if you're considering whether or not to leave school, move across the country, or break up with a long-term partner, you'll want to take your time.

This isn't to say that you need to take things slowly all the time or that you won't ever have to make big decisions under time pressure. The point of learning to walk before you run is to reduce the chance of avoidable negative consequences and make sure you don't speed past options you might not see right away.

Another reason to start slow is to build trust in yourself. When you embrace the process, you let go of needing external validation to confirm every decision you make. You'll need to trust yourself to take the steps that will best support your happiness even when you won't see the results of those steps for months or years.

None of us have gotten this far in life without going through something that made us doubt ourselves. You might not know how to trust yourself right now, but being patient at this stage of change will help you build self-trust.

Stepping outside of your comfort zone is scary. When you're doing something new, you'll be afraid of failing, of losing something, or of making the wrong decision. Trusting yourself to make the best choice you can helps you conquer that fear so it doesn't control you.

The next exercise will help you ask the right questions and assess when to be patient.

EXERCISE: BEING PATIENT

Identify a decision you're facing. Consider the following:

1. Do I have to make this decision right now?
2. What could I stand to gain if I take more time? What could I lose?
3. What could I stand to gain if I hurry? What could I lose?
4. Are there more than two options in this situation?

For a simple assessment like this to be effective, you need to give the questions extended attention. Go back to them over the course of a few days.

A careful, simple step in the right direction is better for your happiness than a big, exciting one in the wrong direction. Taking your time will help you not get stuck or veer off track. Growth only happens outside your comfort zone, so keep up your courage. Learning how to take chances that move you closer to happiness is a skill you will develop if you give yourself time.

LEARNING TO RUN

Being patient is important, but sometimes a chance for growth will pass you by if you don't act quickly. Once you are clear about your purpose, have developed some insight, and have practiced making choices that support your goals, you are ready to seize opportunities when they present.

Where is the line between taking an opportunity and being impulsive? This is a tricky question because the sense of urgency around not wanting to miss something important and around wanting something on the spot looks identical. The only way to tell them apart is understanding the concepts of risk and reward.

People who operate on impulse aren't thinking about growth but rather about immediate gratification. They're operating from a reward mindset with no awareness of possible risks. Again, if it's a smaller decision, like whether or not to buy a pair or shoes or an article of clothing, it's probably not a big deal. However, if it's a bigger decision, like changing your course of study or turning down an internship opportunity, the risks might be significant.

Those who take risks for potential rewards—like taking a job that is beyond their current abilities but offers space to develop new skills—do so because the potential for the change to increase their happiness is a chance worth taking.

After you've practiced evaluating opportunities slowly, it becomes easier to make bigger decisions faster and with more awareness of risk and reward. And by then, you will trust yourself enough to feel confident and commit to the change. Use the next exercise to help you understand how you think and feel about risks and rewards.

EXERCISE: EVALUATING RISK AND REWARD

1. Think of a recent decision you made to turn something down or walk away.

    A. What did you lose by doing this?

    B. What did you gain?

    C. What could you have lost or gained by making a different decision?

    D. Notice the emotions and thoughts associated with your answers.

2. Think of a theoretical growth opportunity that would support your purpose.

    A. What could you lose by taking this?

    B. What could you gain?

    C. Notice the emotions and thoughts associated with your answers.

Noticing how you think and feel about risks and rewards will help you deepen your insight so you can start making bigger decisions on the fly. The more you do this exercise, the more you'll learn about what possibilities are important to you. It can be exhilarating to make a big change. If you've taken the time to learn to run, that excitement will become part of your growing happiness.

TRACKING PROGRESS

Having a record of your gains and losses helps you see the patterns that lead to your success. Your self-care routine, relationships, and hobbies—everything in your daily life— affect how much focus you give to your purpose. The strategy you use also makes a difference. Once you see those connections, you can make smaller changes that support your bigger goals.

For instance, it might be that when you stay up until 2 a.m., you don't have enough focus the next day to put into learning your chosen craft, but it's hard to see this connection without writing it all down. Staying up until 2 a.m. is fun, but is it more important to you than developing a skill that will help you lead a fulfilling life?

Keeping a record also helps you internalize lessons, process your feelings, and notice when you are or aren't using your insight. By writing these things down, you are more likely to notice moments of joy and increases in happiness.

Use the following guide to track your progress toward your goals. You'll need a journal (or a spreadsheet or chart if you like to be highly organized).

EXERCISE: PROGRESSION JOURNAL

1. Write a list of your goals. You can divide them into short-term and long-term if you want to.

2. Record where you're starting with each goal.

3. At the end of every week, write in detail how your week went. Were you tired? Lonely? Excited? Did you do something fun?

4. Also note what you've done to move closer to or further away from each goal. If you haven't made any movement, note that.

5. Do the same thing at the end of each month.

6. Do you notice any patterns? For example, if you were in a low mood for a couple of days, and on those days you didn't make any progress, you've learned something how your mood affects your ability to focus on your purpose.

7. Given this information, what adjustments could you make to your daily life to support your success? How can you best structure your time and energy?

Being mindful of where you are in your journey helps you stay focused on what you need to do to find happiness. And there's joy to be found in seeing how far you've come—think about looking down from the summit of a mountain after an arduous hike.

CHAPTER LEARNINGS

- Learning when you want to fit into society and when you want to stand out leads to greater levels of happiness.
- Knowing how the world's expectations of you do or don't line up with your own values and sense of purpose will help you be true to your own path.
- Finding purpose involves living congruently with your core values and knowing how you want to contribute to the world.
- Pursuing your purpose requires clear intent and motivation.
- As you take new risks, you need to have a place of peace where you can rest and recover.
- Developing insight will help you make the best choices you can in uncertain situations.
- Embracing the process of growth, not just the outcome, is part of becoming happy.
- As you start tackling more important decisions, practice patience to build trust in yourself.
- Learn how to think about risk and reward so you can take bigger chances.
- Track your progress to notice your patterns, learn from mistakes, and appreciate your successes.

A WORLD OF HAPPINESS IN CHAOS

The world hasn't stopped being chaotic just because you've learned some new things about how to navigate it. To keep moving forward, you'll need to think about how to continue applying what you've worked on to your everyday life. You have to stay committed to this process in order to grab onto the hidden happiness that still exists out in the world that not many people find in all of the turmoil out there.

That's what chaotic happiness is all about. Use things that are meant to break you as opportunities to find yourself, find your people, and find your purpose. It's doing all these things that brings you to this paradoxical place of still having to deal with the limitless chaos, yet also feeling profound peace and joy in the midst of it. Once you have this, no one can take it from you. I hope your work in this book has given you a glimpse of your own chaotic happiness, or reminded you that happiness is still possible even if chaos has bogged you down, or you stopped believing in it. So let's talk about how you can continue practicing and living by the three rules of chaotic happiness so that you never forget or stop believing it's possible ever again.

FINDING YOURSELF IN THE UNCHARTED

Finding yourself is about falling in love with building self-awareness and challenging yourself to grow into the person you want to be. This self-discovery work is not one and done. There will always be more to learn about yourself and new opportunities for growth.

For this rule, you had to ask yourself some difficult questions about what's most important to you. You learned about how distorted patterns of thinking get in your way, and you took a look at the current state of your life to start figuring out how to live more authentically. Whether moving through the exercises helped you discover parts of yourself for the first time or reminded you of things you once knew, I hope it was meaningful.

You'll notice that reflecting becomes more natural as you continue to practice the tips from rule #1. You won't need to refer back to the chapter—the work will become part of your everyday routine. When you hit this stage in the process, you'll have internalized the tools and will have them at the ready whenever the world starts to make you feel weary.

As finding yourself becomes easier, you'll start to feel more excitement and less trepidation about living in an uncharted world. When you're unsure what direction to take or have to make a difficult choice, you'll be able to embrace who you are to guide you through the challenge. It's exciting to be able to become a better, stronger version of yourself when life gets hard. That's not to say that the predicaments will be fun, but they will be more meaningful and hold more potential. Remember that to stop exploring defeats the purpose of the rule. If you see that red flag, it's time to revisit the exercises in rule #1.

Above all else, I hope learning how to live by this rule gives you confidence in yourself. You've always been miraculous. With your unique experiences, thoughts and feelings, and sense of self, you offer something special that no one else can. This is the most important part of practicing and living by this rule: a deep appreciation for yourself.

FINDING YOUR PEOPLE IN THE UNPREDICTABLE

Finding your people is about building mutually supportive relationships. The second rule requires vulnerability because it involves taking risks to work on your connections with others. Sometimes the people you find in your life aren't as eager to grow as you are. Even so, working on the dynamics of your relationships—even if it's just how you engage with them— has immense value.

In these exercises, you had to examine your relationships and decide what needed to change. You learned about how to assess the impact people have on your happiness, and you took the time practice assertiveness so that you could set boundaries with the people in your life to protect your happiness. You worked on building empathy, for yourself and for the people you care about the most. Through this exploration, I hope were able to look at your relationships in a different lens and develop the courage to make changes you may never have thought you needed to before.

As you keep working on this rule, you should start to notice more calmness. The more you change your relationships for the better, the more confident you can be in them. When you're confident in your relationships, the unexpected nature of the world becomes less nerve-wracking. No matter what happens, you're surrounded by people who you know will get you through it. You'll find that relying on others' support and care is also deeply rewarding. Over time, being grateful for your people will become as automatic as breathing.

Be careful not to take your progress or your people for granted. Your connections always have room for growth. It's tempting to focus elsewhere when you're feeling comfortable with a certain relationship, but to do so would be a betrayal of an important value: shared meaning. Gratefulness is to meaning as peanut butter is to jelly. Your relationships can't be truly meaningful if you don't express gratitude for them.

You can't control what happens, but you will get through your predicament when you've found the right people to move through the unpredictable challenges. The best way to explain what continued success looks like is a road trip. If you've ever been on a long car ride, then you know that whoever is in the car with you affects the experience. With the wrong people, it can be uncomfortable, long, boring, and especially uneasy if the weather is bad. When you're with the right people, time flies. It's like being home away from home, and the unpredictability the weather brings, much like life, is substantially less daunting.

I hope you discovered how much people need you, too, while working through this chapter. Being grateful for what you give others, as well as appreciating what they give to you, makes the unpredictable world less intimidating.

FINDING YOUR PURPOSE IN THE UNCERTAIN

The last rule, finding your purpose, is the most existentially challenging one and can be harder to wrap your head around. It takes years for many people to figure this out, and rightfully so. Deciding what you want to dedicate your life to is not something to take lightly. What is most meaningful to you needs to be able to motivate you. If it doesn't, what's the point?

These exercises helped you look at how you spend your time now. Is what you put energy into just a way to get by, or does it have the potential to help you lead a fulfilling life? You needed to evaluate what is important to you and how you want to participate in the world. Not only that, but you considered how to intentionally act on your purpose while also ensuring that you keep yourself motivated and stable. Lastly, you learned how to pace yourself so you don't burn out through this process.

As you focus more on finding your purpose, you should start to develop a sixth sense for what is a real motivator and what isn't. You will also start to notice that living with purpose can be thrilling. Purpose is like the keys to a Ferrari that only you get to drive—having this special source of adrenaline is satisfying. Uncertainty of outcome is no longer something to fear. Even if you fail, you have a limitless supply of fuel—purpose—that keeps you engaged in meaningful effort.

Make sure to keep believing in the magic of this rule. It's easy for our day-to-day life to lose its luster and for us to start seeing our existence as arbitrary and mundane. But the only reason we see things this way is because we forget that purpose isn't the same as outcomes—it can't be lost.

I hope you've come to see that you have the agency to live a purpose-filled life. The world doesn't get to dictate what you care about. Life isn't fair, but life is what you make it. When you work to develop your own purpose, you take your happiness into your own hands rather than letting the world decide for you what it means.

PACING YOURSELF

Knowing how to pace yourself as you move through the rules of chaotic happiness and when to revisit certain exercises or topics will help you build the foundation for long-lasting happiness. To figure out what pace is right for you, start by reviewing what we've already talked about. Based on your answers to the questions in this next exercise—the last exercise!—you may want to reread certain chapters and spend more time with certain exercises. Remember that the principles of each rule—finding yourself, finding your people, and finding your purpose—are all part of being happy.

EXERCISE: THE RIGHT PACE

1. **Rule #1: Find Yourself**

   A. As you worked through the chapter and exercises, how confident did you feel?

   B. Which exercises did you have trouble finishing?

   C. Do you have a clear sense of the person you want to become?

   D. If not, what questions do you still have?

   E. How will you know when you've mastered the skills outlined in this chapter?

2. **Rule #2: Find Your People**

   A. As you worked through the chapter and exercises, how confident did you feel?

   B. Which exercises did you have trouble finishing?

   C. Do you know what changes you need to make so your relationships are more satisfying and supportive?

   D. If not, which ones are you feeling stuck with? Why?

   E. How will you know when you've mastered the skills outlined in this chapter?

3. **Rule #3: Find Your Purpose**

   A. As you worked through the chapter and exercises, how confident did you feel?

   B. Which exercises did you have trouble finishing?

   C. Do you have a clear sense of what your purpose is?

   D. If not, what's in the way? Too many options, no options that you can see, no excitement about what you've come up with?

   E. How will you know when you've mastered the skills outlined in this chapter?

By looking at what you've covered, you should be able to tell where you might want to keep working before you move on to the next section of the book. And remember: embrace the process! You've already started.

CHAOTIC HAPPINESS

I want to thank you for learning with me and send you off with a few parting thoughts about chaotic happiness.

Chaotic happiness doesn't mean that chaos makes you happy, or even that you can be happy despite the chaos. It means that our deepest happiness is often the result of our deepest struggles. To experience true chaotic happiness, you have to take on life's challenges.

I believe happiness is just as likely to come from chaos as suffering is. Hear me out on this. This chaos we live in—is it a challenge or is it a calling? The more I work through these rules for myself, the more I see it as the second.

To be happy and to find it in our most difficult challenges calls us to love our life more broadly than before. We're not picking and choosing which moments are meaningful; we're saying yes to all of it in its seeming imperfection.

It's profoundly fulfilling to search for happiness in the world because there are deeply challenging aspects of life that get in the way. After the reflecting you've done, have you started to see it this way, too?

Life is heartbreaking and rewarding at the same time. The process of finding chaotic happiness is no different. Remember this if nothing else: the world may be lost to the chaos, but our humanity and happiness are not.

May your happiness increase with every challenge you face. May you always have the courage to keep fighting for it despite daunting circumstances.

Thanks for reading.

INDEX

ABOUT THE AUTHOR

TJ Hoegh, MS, NCC, LPC, is a licensed therapist from Hampton, Iowa. He received his BA from Grand View University and his MS from Minnesota State University at Mankato. He practices individual and family psychotherapy in the suburbs of Chicago. In his free time, TJ enjoys spending time with family and friends, as well as educating people about their mental health. He is known internationally for the latter on TikTok, where he has amassed millions of followers.

ACKNOWLEDGMENTS

First and foremost, I'd like to thank the team of people at DK who collaborated with me to create this book: Alexandra Andrzejewski, Jessica Lee, William Thomas, Mike Sanders, Augustin Kendall, Kristen Fisher, Kelsey Curtis, Yiffy Gu, Georgette Beatty, Lorraine Martindale, Beverlee Dee, and countless others.

On a more personal note, I'd like to thank my family: Jane and Scott Hoegh, Marilyn and James Jensen, Phyllis and Calvin Hoegh, Alexis Vosburg, Zach Vosburg, Isaac Vosburg, William Vosburg, Travis Hoegh, Kirsten Hoegh, Soren Hoegh, Ingrid Hoegh, Payton Hoegh, Jazmin Hoegh, Kara Hoegh, Dexter Hoegh, and Balto Hoegh.

I'd also like to thank my close friends: Mackenzie Baack, Mitch Vetter, Drew Heuberger, Chance Rhodes, Chris Huling, Treyton Craig, and Miguel Vega.

Lastly, I'd like to thank my colleagues and educators who shared their knowledge with me throughout the years: Dr. Diane Coursol, Dr. Karen Lindstrom, Dr. Ann Miller, Dr. John Seymour, Dr. Tracy Peed, Dr. Helena Stevens, Dr. Rick Auger, Dr. David Hall, Jessica Shouler, Charley Smith, Jimena Escurra, Christine Hazelett, Lauren Schifferdecker, and Lauren Madden.

Publishing this book wouldn't have been possible without the support and care I've received from the above people. I'm forever grateful to you.